MORTGAGE STORM

Making It Rain By Mastering Your Craft

Million Dollar Tips From Top Producers and Coaches

Any trademarks mentioned in this book are listed for reference purposes only and are the property of the respective trademark owners.

Table of Contents

INTRODUCTION 1

BRAD ROCHE 3

BARRY HABIB 17

VINNIE APOSTOLICO................................. 33

DOUGLAS BATEMAN 45

JASON REDMAN 59

ALEX CARAGIANNIDES........................... 73

SHERREE MONTERO 85

RICHARD LYTLE.................................. 97

DEANN ELLIS....................................... 109

JOEL COMP...................................... 121

BRAD COHEN..................................... 131

JASON GOSSER 143

JUSTIN OLIVER 157

JOE MCBREEN................................. 169

JJ MAZZO 181

MANUEL CORRAL.................................... 193

Introduction

....

The mortgage origination profession can be one of the most rewarding careers in the sales field. Generally income is commission-based and the earning potential is only limited by individual performance. As with most sales professionals, there is a wide range of performance and thus level of success and income varies greatly. Whereas the average mortgage professional earns in the mid five figures according to published statistics, the authors in this book have mastered their craft and have figured out the path to achievement that results in earnings well into the six figures and even seven figures. On a combined basis the authors have originated over $20 billion of residential mortgages over their careers.

We have brought together sixteen top producing mortgage professionals from around the United States as co-authors of this book. Although they are all in the top tier of their industry, they have willingly shared their individual insights so others in the industry can benefit from what they have learned along the way. Many of our authors have been speakers at major national or regional mortgage and real estate conferences and seminars and many of them give back to the industry by providing coaching programs.

The authors tell the stories of their individual paths to success and how they have overcome adversity and endured difficult market conditions. All of the authors have overcome obstacles along the way and they lay out the most common challenges facing new mortgage originators and loan offices in the current era after the financial meltdown and new regulatory environment.

The authors opine on the keys to success in the mortgage industry and there are some common themes in the tips offered. Maintaining high ethical standards, building a business based on trust, having the proper mindset, and a focus on providing an exceptional level of customer service are echoed throughout the book as imperatives. A common challenge in any sales function is acquiring customers and the authors share their strategies that lead to finding new customers as well as repeat and referral business. They also share how they have developed their branding and marketing to stand out from the crowded field of competitors in what can be generally considered a commodity business. Finally, personal efficiency and organization, as well as building an effective team, are indicated as critical to be able to continuously grow the business.

The publisher wants to thank Brad Roche of Mortgage Planner Marketing, who is one of the authors. Brad worked with us to come up with the book concept and title. Being a well-connected top producer, coach, and national speaker in the mortgage industry, Brad recommended the inclusion of the majority of our authors who are all top mortgage producers as well as coaches and speakers.

Brad Roche

Introduction

While growing up in Michigan, my father had his own residential mortgage company. I got an early start, working part-time in his company during my junior year in high school. I initially helped with several marketing tasks and put together first-time homebuyer workbooks. Eventually I went into processing mortgages, helping clients through the process. I also obtained my CHUMS No. with FHA to underwrite. Then I became an assistant loan originator, working with my dad. He was a great mentor and I could not imagine a better way to get into the business. I worked my way up to being partner in the company and eventually took over full responsibility for the business. In addition to being a mortgage loan officer for the past twenty-three years, I have also been a licensed real estate agent for ten years and was a lead developer for commercial and residential property developments. I also spent ten years as a mortgage coach with The Core Training during my development as a loan officer.

We established our presence in the Charlotte, North Carolina area in 2010 and I'm a mortgage banker covering the Carolinas. In addition to my work as a top producing mortgage originator, I'm coaching a select group of mortgage loan officers from around the United States.

Common Obstacles for Loan Officers

Getting Experience to Know the Deal

The money can be real great for originators and new people in the business want to go right into to originating, but are just winging it. You don't know what you don't know. There's an art to knowing your deal, knowing what you can charge, what you can't charge, what makes sense for the borrower to pay, what doesn't, what loans make sense, and really listening to the borrower's goals so that you are putting them in the right product at the right time in their life. That's a huge piece that I think a lot of new and some experienced originators miss. You can't learn this in college or any other school, except by getting the experience working under someone who has that experience. Not only does this help win the deal from your competition, but also it is in the best interest of the client—knowing cost vs. fee breakeven points and goals.

Originators have to pass a test to get their license, but nothing on the test asked anything about what type of loan to put borrowers in, based on their goals or financial aspirations that they're after. I think that piece alone is what's most vital for a loan officer being successful. This is a business where success follows people that provide the best advice and service to their clients.

Mortgages by Themselves Are a Commodity, but Mortgage Origination Should Be a Value-added Service

Many people in this business get stuck because the thing they are selling a commodity. We all have very similar programs and products, wherever you go. If a borrower calls enough people, somebody is going to have a lower rate than we are; there's always going to be someone cheaper. So, what is it that gives value to what you do? It sounds like a cliché, but you've got to create a value-added service to make yourself more desirable than the next mortgage originator. When someone is shopping

4

for a mortgage, they're shopping for a rate, they're shopping for cost, but they're also shopping to see who has the confidence to be able to provide the best mortgage for their unique situation. Purchasing a house is a very stressful undertaking and they are also looking for someone that can effectively serve them and get the mortgage closed in time.

Value of Mentors and Coaches

There is tremendous value in working under a successful loan officer as you are getting started in the mortgage industry. My mentor was my dad who was a great loan officer and I was able to work side-by-side with him for a number of years. I started assisting on mortgage processing when I was only nineteen years old. A lot of originators want to get started in the business without paying the dues and learning all that is needed to put the right deal for the client together. There's an art to knowing the deal. I'd advise new loan officers to start out as an assistant to work with someone who's closing fifteen, twenty, or more loans a month, like I was able to do. You don't want to be trying to learn from the typical loan officer, closing only three to five loans a month. By working with the successful originator, you'll be looking at sixty to a hundred credit reports per month and analyzing what loan product makes the most sense for the clients; if they qualify or they don't qualify; and how to process the loans. That's experience you can't get any other way and by picking the right originator to work with, your knowledge base will grow many times faster.

Then when you finally graduate from being an assistant after a couple years, you will have built your strength and you will understand an important concept and the first rule I learned in the business, "Know Your Deal." I have a plaque in my office to this day to always remind me that says, "Know Your Deal." That means knowing that a client would choose you because you're advising them with better advice than anyone else and you feel confident about what loan you're putting them into.

I also was coached for a few years by The Core Training and then I worked with them for over ten years as a coach while being a loan officer. I found out that you learn a lot by teaching other people, as well. While I was being coached, I was taught the bigger pile principle. The person that is a big achiever in a specific field has the most to teach in that field. You don't go to the gym and learn how to get fit from an overweight person. It doesn't make sense. If you are going to be coached in the mortgage field, find a coach who is at the level you aspire to, or is close to that level. Absolutely listen to your coach and do what your coach tells you to do. Don't change what you are told to do until you get to your teacher's level and you have mastered it. Do what they tell you to do, achieve similar results and then make it better. That's where it becomes mastering your craft.

A lot of originators try to cut through and not go after mastering what they set out for; they're taking the short cut. It's that bigger pile principle where you get involved with someone who's doing more than you are and you learn how to perform up to that level and then go past that level. You don't question how they got there, where you want to be, or close to where you want to be. Listen to your coach and do exactly what your coach tells you to do. If someone has a million dollars in the bank and you want a million dollars in the bank, learn how they got a million dollars and copy it. Don't argue or disagree with what they tell you until you're past that million.

Keys to Success As a Mortgage Originator

Use Excellent Service As a Differentiator

The biggest typical complaint in the industry from clients is that they are going through the entire process and that they're not getting updated during the processing. It's generally a nervous time because of closing deadlines. I recommend that you establish systems so that you can make routine, scheduled updates to clients and the real estate agents involved in the transaction.

We put a system in place some years ago so that every Tuesday, by noon, clients and their agents receive an updated status on their loan. It's in writing, and with the update, they know exactly where they are in the lending process and they don't have to call us to find the status. That has completely taken away that complaint.

The second typical complaint about the mortgage industry is that the client is surprised at closing. Here again, this is easy to solve by getting clients accurate preliminary closing statements early in the process. There have been many improvements in regulations and compliance to minimize the surprises at closing; however, we have gone beyond requirements by providing the exact cost information right up front. All the sample documents are sent way ahead of closing so that there are no surprises when they get there.

Develop a Cross-selling Platform That Provides Value-added Benefits to Clients

When we moved and set up in the Charlotte area in 2010, we had to establish our client base from nothing. It was also not a very robust time from an economy standpoint. By setting up a cross-selling platform we were able to become the preferred lender at a number of businesses in the area and a the same time we were able to offer our clients some value-added services that also helped attract typical referral partners, like real estate and insurance agents, CPAs, and financial planners. Because of the unique things we offered, we rapidly gained a lot of referrals and in the first year of business in the area we closed about 170 loans.

Most loan officers don't have anything except for their loan programs and rates. If you can develop something that doesn't cost anything but can provide value to your clients, you are one step ahead. As we were meeting with businesses and becoming the preferred lender for their employees, we discussed with the businesses about making free or discount offers to our clients. This is really a way for businesses to let our clients sample their services and a lot of the time that brings in additional sales for our business partners.

This was developed into a welcome package we now call "Passport to Charlotte." The businesses give us discounts or free offers that we package together. Some examples are free or discounted beverages, meals, hotel stays, car rentals, and so on. We even have a free first lawn cutting service after clients close on the new home. We also provide our brochure in the package so the clients can get to know us better. We start out offering benefits as soon as the loan is pre-approved.

Develop a System to Maximize Referrals Starting During the Mortgage Process

We do things during the process that make us unique and get our clients to tell their friends and family about their experience, which is truly how to get referrals. It's the excellent service level and benefits we provide that makes working with us an experience, instead of just the transaction they get with other lenders. It's the experience that makes them want to refer.

In the mortgage business I was trained that there are four pages to an application. The first page is your name, address, Social

Security Number. The second page has your income and assets. The third page has the declarations that the clients answer. The fourth page is blank. I was always taught that's the area that you fill in as you're talking with your client. Who's your CPA? Who's your financial planner? Who is your insurance agent? Do you have anyone at work that you know that will be buying a new home?

You create opportunities on page four to get referrals. If they're happy with their CPA, financial planner and insurance agent, you can introduce yourself to them, telling them you are working with their client. Then you can try to set up an introductory meeting that may ultimately result in a new referral partner, especially after the client describes your excellent service. If the client is not happy with one of their service providers, you have the opportunity to refer the client to one of your current referral partners, solidifying that relationship.

I have seen statistics that if you can get a referral from a client during the processing of their transaction, 60% of the time the client will refer business in the future while you are conducting other campaigns. Unfortunately if you don't get a referral during the process, your chance of getting a referral down the road decreases to 20%. Since the opportunity of future referrals is three times higher if we get a referral while we are processing their loan, we want to maximize this opportunity.

One way to do this is to give the client opportunities to thank us. There are a number of ways to create this opportunity, but superior service, like the weekly updates, is one of the ways. It is important for the loan officer and team to have a "referral reflex." When the client calls you or one of your team, thanking you for your service or for something you are doing for them, there should be an automatic response, like a reflex. The reflex response needs to be thought out and should be aimed at getting a specific response relating to a referral, something like, "I appreciate you noticing that. Thank you so much for picking us because we know you have a lot of choices for a lender. Who is the next person most likely to purchase or refinance? You are a great customer and we would like to get more customers just like you." If they don't know of anyone, ask if they can help you get a discussion with their employer to become the preferred lender at their employer's business.

When a client gets pre-approved, they're all excited about the transaction. One of the most exciting times for them is that moment when they finally get their offer accepted, maybe even more than when they get the key. When their offer is accepted we send them a huge box of gourmet popcorn delivered to their office. We send it to their office as a way of saying thank you for choosing us because we know you had a lot of choices. We also do it so that they tell their friends, family, and especially their co-workers, who are also there enjoying the gift, how great we were and that experience we're giving to them. This is another way to generate referrals during the process.

Develop Your Personal Branding and Positioning so You Become Known As the Mortgage Expert in Your Market

This is really part of the cold marketing everyone should be doing to some extent, again so that you stand out from other loan officers and provide something more than just programs and rates. Today, you're not likely to have much difference in products with your competitors, and if you are just marketing on rates and programs, you're going to be very limited in your ability to offer anything unique or special.

One of the things I recommend is to have a brand for your origination business apart from the lender that you represent. As I example I am known as "The Mortgage Planner," and I have developed a following and a website around this brand. You need to have some kind of a draw that makes you more attractive to do business with than just being another loan officer. I mentioned earlier how we developed the "Passport To Charlotte" program,

10

that not only benefits our clients by offering savings from local businesses, but the businesses that participate are able to benefit with incremental business opportunities by participating.

Another thing you can do is to develop a niche around an activity or a business where you have a passion about more than just the loan business. You can become the go-to lender for this niche that you have an affinity for.

One of my coaching students used to work for an airline. He started positioning himself as "Mortgage Flights" and he makes a special effort to market to airline personnel. This has gotten him lots of business from people in that industry. He has been able to get his information into break rooms and has gotten very well known at the airlines. With a large presence in this one industry he has been able to go market himself to other referral partners. He has a great audience so more and more referral partners want to work with him.

Another loan officer has a huge love for baseball. He used to play baseball and both of his kids play in youth baseball. He's marketed himself as "Home Run Mortgage." He sponsors a lot of Little League teams and he's at the games letting parents know what he does. He put some extra effort into marketing to baseball parents and he is getting tons of people referring him from that source.

The list can go on and on. My passion was small businesses and that's why I developed "Passport to Charlotte" and became the preferred lender for small to medium sized business, which can give the benefit of a lower cost to their employees. One of the best things you can do is go to the local places that you love and ask to become a preferred lender and start networking in those areas.

Another thing that is very powerful is using the media to position you as the expert. I've got a weekly radio show that is carried on four stations in the Carolinas. This really separates me from all of the other loan officers out there. Having a broadcast radio show definitely positions you as an expert in the market because you are sharing a lot of tips and ways to navigate the process. Radio has allowed me to help people get a better plan together and to avoid some of the pitfalls. This also lets the referral partners know that I know the process and I know how to get the client navigated through it. Again, it's knowing your deal. I have also tried to position myself so that I get noticed and the news media has sought me out and I have been quoted in numerous media.

Although I don't do much advertising, the right type of advertising can also help get attention. I generally advertise with a full-page ad in a high-end real estate publication where the other advertisers are mostly top producing agents. I'm generally the only lender in that publication.

Get a Great Mentor or Coach to Accelerate Your Business Progress

A final piece of advice is to get a great mentor or a coach to start you out. I didn't go to college, but I kind of went through a boot camp under the mentorship of my dad who was a top producer. I participated in a coaching program for several years and it just made me better. A coach of mine said, "If you hang around dogs you're going to get fleas. Hang around eagles, you're going to learn to fly." Be sure to surround yourself with top performers and you'll be able to copy systems and do similar things and achieve similar results, in less time.

I have been giving back by coaching others for a number of years, initially through a national training company and then more recently with my own coaching business and I've been able to watch students go up by eight to fifteen million dollars in production each year. Most of this is by being efficient and applying and leveraging systems to outperform the other guys out there. We all have the same 24 hours in a day, but successful people use the time better than everyone else.

When you hire a coach and you pay the coach, your attitude is to grow and learn. I do think that the key is to doing it quickly and speed of implementation is huge. Also make sure the new systems you are setting up are going to stick. You can implement a lot of things but they will go away after a while if you quit following them. You'll then be back as square one. You need to create habits and rituals to make the new systems stay in place so you don't go backwards.

About Brad Roche

Brad Roche is known among the Charlotte area real estate industry as "The Mortgage Planner." He has been a mortgage loan officer for over twenty-three years and consistently ranks in the Top 1% in the United States for loan originations. He is a mortgage banker and area manager, affiliated with Element Funding, where he is responsible for four offices in the Carolinas. His experience in addition to mortgage lending also includes ten years as a licensed real estate agent, ten years as a mortgage sales trainer with a national training organization and lead developer on multi-million dollar commercial and residential projects. He is also coaching Mortgage Planning Systems to a select group of mortgage originators nationwide.

Brad has packaged his mortgage origination success formula and systems and is making them available to loan originators that want to grow their business, whether they are just starting out, or are experienced loan officers. The complete system is called, "Before, During, and After," which refers to the business success growth strategies that are applied at each stage of mortgage client engagement. A set of tools, systems and strategies are provided for each stage that create and automatically connect with referral partners and guarantee client satisfaction beyond the norms of the mortgage industry.

Brad is a frequent speaker and was a keynote speaker at the Real Estate and Mortgage Mastermind Summit in 2015 and 2016. He is also a bestselling author and has a weekly radio show focusing on mortgages that is broadcast in North and South Carolina by four stations including CBS, Fox and ESPN. He was named among National Mortgage Professional Magazine's 40 Most Influential Mortgage Professionals Under 40 for 2015.

For more information about Brad Roche, visit http://www.TheMortgagePlanner.net.

For more information about the "Before, During, and After" system, visit http://www.MortgagePlannerMarketing.com.

MORTGAGE STORM

Barry Habib

....

Introduction

Not too many people in the mortgage industry planned to be in this business originally, and like most, I got into the industry by accident. At a young age, I started to purchase some real estate properties as investments. Some of them I flipped, some of them I fixed up and sold, and some of them I retained and rented out. I needed mortgages on all these different properties so I got to know a number of the mortgage professionals in the area. I asked one of them how the business worked and what some of the top guys earned. I was pretty impressed with the earnings potential and felt I could do a great job helping people get mortgage financing. I had gone to college for finance and economics and was always good with math, so I thought it would be a good fit.

It was a good thing I was inexperienced and didn't know how difficult this business was going to be, because maybe I would have been scared out of it, but I took a leap of faith and got started. I realized right away that it was going to take some extra effort and I did some unconventional things to start bringing in business.

I would tell everyone I spoke to that I was in the mortgage business. In fact, at night, I would knock on people's doors and ask them if they wanted to refinance. In my third week in the mortgage business, I wrote sixteen loans. A lot of mortgage professionals never wrote sixteen loans in a week or even in a month. It was really a great way to get a start building a business. I'm in New Jersey and whenever I went on the turnpike or on a toll bridge I'd always go to where there was a toll collector and hand them my card. This was in the days before E-Z Pass and those automated mechanisms that you just drive through. Even if I had exact change, I'd go to the lane with a toll collector. My friends used to give me a little bit of razzing about it, because I would delay things. Before too long one of the toll collectors called me up and, not only did I do his loan, but I did seventeen for his friends as well. It just goes to show, if you think outside of the box, there are ways to accomplish things that others might find a little bit more difficult.

I've been involved in the mortgage industry for thirty years now, starting as a mortgage loan originator. Currently, I'm the CEO of MBS Highway, a company and platform created to help interpret and forecast activity in the mortgage rate and bond markets. One of my career highlights was being recognized for having the highest annual mortgage origination production in the United States on two different occasions.

Lessons From Life and Business – Building Trust and Alleviating Points of Friction

I grew up incredibly poor. I was fighting the odds from the beginning because my parents were much older. They were immigrants and my dad was 57 when I was born. It was a good thing Rowe vs. Wade was not enacted when I was born; otherwise, I wouldn't be here. So, I'm on bonus time here. Growing up very poor was enlightening. I was a very happy kid but it kind of forced me to be more creative and to explore other ways to improve.

At a very early age I started a stereo business by selling stereo equipment out of the trunk of my car. I approached people cold and asked them if they wanted to purchase stereo equipment. That taught me a lot of life lessons about needing to speak to people and understand that the more you speak to people the more your chances improve. But it also taught me an understanding about building trust. As in all industries, things go wrong and a few of the pieces of equipment I sold didn't work properly when the customer got home. When someone purchases stereo equipment from a kid selling it out of the trunk of a car, they never expect to see him again and never expect to get a response if they called.

Contrary to their expectations, when something went wrong with their equipment, I would either exchange or repair it and do the right thing. What I discovered was that in almost every single situation the customer went from being disappointed about the incident and the problem to being incredibly impressed with the fact that I was truly concerned and could be trusted. They felt obligated to either tell other people about me or buy more equipment themselves just because of the law of reciprocity. At a young age I discovered that problems could really be a blessing if handled properly. They help build trust because when things are great, everything is easy and everybody thinks they trust you. But when something goes wrong, it's how you handle the problems that either build the trust or destroys it.

Once I got in the mortgage business it was the same thing. There were a lot of instances where something went wrong processing the loan and even today the mortgage business is a somewhat a problem business. There are a whole host of things that could go wrong that are out of our control as loan officers. They are not our fault, but it makes it very easy to hide and bury them when you don't have answers and are being pressured by the real estate agents and the borrower. Some may think they don't have an answer, so they're not going to get back to them. It's those individuals who step up, are accessible, and are there every step of the way that have longevity and build the trust when things go wrong. Embrace those difficult situations because you will be building trust for the future. It's a very important and valuable lesson for us to learn.

The other thing to do is consider the repetitive things that go wrong in a business and either develop systems and processes to improve the customer experience or to better lay out and communicate the appropriate expectation level. In this way we can attempt to alleviate those points of friction, improving our customer's experience, building trust, and creating raving fans in the process. That concept has carried through to every industry that I've been in.

Back in the early '90s I discovered that the mortgage industry had no real representation on TV. The media was always bashing the mortgage industry and cast us as the bad guys. Talk about a big point of friction in the media. I decided to stand up and represent the mortgage industry by doing educational TV spots. I started on CNBC and then later at CNN, FOX, and Bloomberg. I was kind of the voice of the mortgage industry, articulating the reality during the times of the financial crisis where everyone was pointing fingers at us, but it really wasn't the mortgage originator's fault.

I was the lone wolf out there who explained that although it's not as if there are no bad actors, there certainly are, but the bulk of the people in the mortgage industry are good people. The big cause of the problems was the credit rating agencies and the greed factor on Wall Street that had put us in this position. Mortgage originators didn't invent the crazy loan programs that became commonplace. Even if an originator advised their customer not to choose an aggressive mortgage product, and the customer demanded the product, often the originator was blamed for putting them into a product when they defaulted.

Even in other industries I've found that alleviating points of friction helps build trust and creates a better customer experience. I had a medical imaging business that not only did MRIs, but also some leading edge scans like cardio endoscopy and PET/CTs to detect cancer early. I hope that people reading this never have to go for some of these scary things. But if you have, or know somebody that has, you can certainly relate. People going for the scans generally have a lot of anxiety and the bad point is you have to wait until your doctor gets the results and schedules an appointment with you to know the outcome. Human nature is that we always think the worst, we worry about the results and for a few days until we get to see our doctor we're nervous about it.

Now the reality is the technician doing the scans knows what's going on and has the experience but is not allowed to let the patient know the results. We tried to alleviate that anxiety which is point of friction by putting a radiologist right there at the imaging center. By the time the patient is finished getting dressed, the radiologist had the scans up and would sit with the patient. If it was great news, great, if it's not such great news, the patient had a plan of action as to what to do and we eliminated the anxiety portion of it. People responded very well to our solution and it became a successful business that I sold.

I was the lead producer and managing partner for "Rock of Ages," which was the 27th longest running show in the history of Broadway. Besides producing, one of the things that I did was alleviate a common point of friction on Broadway. Many people going to Broadway shows enjoy a cocktail before the show or during intermission, but when the show starts or resumes they had to either chug the drink or leave it because drinks were not allowed inside the theatre. I thought that was an unnecessary point of friction.

I asked the theatre owner, "Why don't we let these people have their drinks in the seats?" The owner said, "No, we've never done that before. Nobody does that on Broadway." Well, that's not a good enough answer for me. I fought, and fought, and became the first show in the history of Broadway to allow drinking in the seats. Now all of them do it.

I've seen people in the mortgage industry getting re-priced, losing locks, not understanding the market and losing transactions to people who were better educated on the financial markets. I decided to create products to help originators become better educated and better able to articulate what's happening in the markets and to gain the confidence of the potential buyer or potential referral source. In this way they can increase, so to speak, their batting average, which is converting more of the opportunities that they have been given. This is another example of looking at obstacles as points of friction and turning them into opportunities, if we can alleviate them. That's what we try to do every single day with MBS Highway. We try to understand what are the points of friction that originators have and alleviate them so that the originator can alleviate the agent's points of friction as well as the customer's.

Common Obstacles for Loan Officers

You Have to Be Knowledgeable to Maintain Compliance

Regulations and underwriting guidelines were much more flexible when I was originating full-time. After the big financial meltdown of 2007 to 2009, regulations tightened significantly and the entire mortgage industry entered a new era. It has since became more of a challenge to qualify for a mortgage and lenders have had to be much more educated so they can provide proper advice to borrowers. Originators need to be incredibly detail oriented and have a good understanding of all of the complicated compliance requirements.

Technology Has Made Information a Commodity and of Less Value Than in the Past

Today's technology makes a lot of things easier, but technology's also a double-edged sword because it lowers the barrier to entry to other competitors that we didn't have in the past. I think that now and going forward, we have to understand that Millennials are going to be driving a lot of the activity, much like baby-boomers did for a long time. Millennials grew up with Google in their hand, so they don't need information. They'll give you the answer to a question before you finish asking it.

What we really have to understand is that Millennials need, in fact, what everyone needs, is wisdom and insight as opposed to just information. Originators that focus on providing information will have a more difficult time going forward than those who focus on building a knowledge base that allows them to properly advise borrowers. That starts with understanding that while we call our industry the mortgage business, it's truly the money business. Nobody really wants a mortgage, what they want is money, and the mortgage is just the mechanism that pays it back over time. We have to understand how money works and that money is multi-faceted.

A mortgage is typically the single largest financial transaction an individual makes, but it also touches every aspect of their financial plan, from cash flow and monthly payments, to the asset they're purchasing. It could be a huge wealth creation tool or provide the ability to maximize tax benefits. It also impacts retirement planning and college savings. That's why the mortgage originator going forward has to be able to view themselves as having a large knowledge base and an understanding of the multiple aspects of the money business, as opposed to just the mortgage itself. The mortgage originator of yesterday is somebody who does a really good job of understanding their guidelines and qualifying and today we can automate qualifying. What you have to do now are the things that automation cannot do—understanding the needs of your customers and helping them make the best financial choices. The originators that can do that, in my opinion, will do exceptionally well.

Keys to Success As a Mortgage Originator

Have a Tough Mindset

You have to have a really tough mindset to be successful in this industry. The mortgage business is a great business, but it's also a problem business. Lots of things are out of your control that can make you look bad. Whether it's on the legal side, something on the appraisal side, whatever it is, there will be problems that occur, and you're going to be the one to blame and you're also going to be the quarterback that's got to pull it all together. It's a very hard business and you need to be resilient, resourceful, and always stay a step ahead. Those that don't have that tough mentality are going to have a difficult time lasting in this industry.

Be Goal Oriented

Goal orientation is also incredibly important to your success. Your primary competition has to simply be yourself and the standards you set for yourself. You have to set goals and you have to measure performance against your goals because what gets measured gets done. Set realistic goals, but ones that stretch you and cause you to reach out of your comfort zone and push yourself beyond that. This will give you motivation and it also gives you a reason to make a few extra calls, stay a little bit later, and push yourself to that next level. Goal setting is an extraordinarily powerful tool. If you don't set goals, you're just going to be floundering. You're just taking what you're getting and that's not a very productive way to move forward.

Differentiate Yourself by Becoming the Source of Wisdom and Insight Instead of Just the Provider of Information

You have to think about the value you can provide that is not easily replicated by technology. Knowing the guidelines for a loan is an important thing, but that's the price of admission. It's not going to make you excel and it's no longer a competitive advantage. The competitive advantage is being able to understand the financial markets, articulate them correctly, and really make a difference in your customer's financial future. It's not just by getting them a mortgage, but by getting them THE mortgage that makes a positive influence on their life. It's locking their rate in at the correct time, helping them choose the correct program, suggests the correct loan amount and making sure that the collateral that they're using has been properly evaluated so that they understand their opportunity.

Do we have great data to understand the financial and housing markets and the future expectations for appreciation? What would the impact of certain appreciation levels be on the asset that they're purchasing? These are the things that are going to get a customer excited. How much of a mortgage can they take? Understanding what they would do with additional cash, or less cash. What would it do to their tax situation? What would this mean for their kids' college education, or their retirement planning? What are their future goals? When do they think they're going to be out of this property? What product should they choose? Only 5% of transactions are adjustable rate mortgages in today's market, but is a fixed or an adjustable rate the right decision?

When we look at today's landscape, understanding that there is potentially a high probability of a recession occurring in the next few years, why would somebody not take a serious look at an adjustable rate mortgage (ARM), when knowing that in recessionary periods, interest rates decline rather precipitously. The borrower could have opportunities to maximize cash flow and maximize the ability to either use the difference between the savings of an adjustable rate and a fixed rate to pay down the mortgage. The difference in payments that you make between the two, over the period before the first adjustment of the ARM, generates a significant guaranteed return on investment, much higher than typical investments can earn. How many originators know that? How many agents know that? How many customers benefit? That's what I mean by being able to give advice that is far superior to your competitors.

The great thing is that financial markets are always changing, so if you can understand the moves, you are able to stay ahead of your competition and always be able to have something new and exciting to provide to your customers. Another thing you might consider is getting a securities license. It's a big commitment, but it definitely gives you a very good background.

Your knowledge base also helps when working with referral sources like real estate agents and builders. What they really would love for us to do is not just to quote a rate or get the mortgage done, but also to provide them additional value or tools that help them close transactions. If we were able to truly articulate the opportunity that exists in the housing market and help the agent market that and let the customer see what the value of different levels of appreciation are and what the customer can benefit from, then of course they would want to work with us. It doesn't matter who they were working with in the past.

MBS Highway is a subscription-based platform where we provide our students with an understanding of the financial markets, and more importantly, we help them articulate that knowledge to their customers. We have a series of tools that allows them to be a better resource to the borrower, the real estate agent, the builder, and anyone else involved in the transaction. In addition to these tools, I post a new coaching video every day to keep our students up to date with the latest market trends.

In addition to being able to give thorough advice to your clients, I also think it's very important to be able to give presentations. There's nothing like being up in front of a group of people and being in that authoritative position, and then delivering very valuable content. It makes the audience think, "Wow, this person obviously knows what they're talking about. I need to know more of that." Your audience would then be more likely to gravitate towards you and want to learn more from you, and do more business with you. Although public speaking is a great way to position yourself as the expert, there have been a number of surveys resulting in the conclusion that speaking in front of an audience is one of the scariest things that individuals face in their life. The reason it's scary is because you're not sure what to say or you don't know if the audience will like it. You question whether you will be able to prepare the presentation in an articulate manner.

One of the tools we provide at MBS highway is the Presentation Expressway, which includes presentations that I make in small bite-sized pieces so it's easy for our students to grasp the content. I record the presentations so you can listen to me deliver them. We prepare everything for presenters, including the PowerPoint slides, so they can just learn it, rehearse it, and they can go out and deliver a winning presentation every time.

Even if you are a relatively new originator, you can still position yourself as an expert in the market. Armed with knowledge, you can be a source of information to news media who are always starved for fresh content. You can come in with your great content and they print it. Now you've got a reputation for being an expert because you have been quoted or featured in the media. You use that in your marketing and create instant credibility because you're coming in as the expert.

You Need to Have Great Organization Skills

Organizational skills are paramount, because this is a problem business. It's much easier to keep a good reputation than it is to try and repair a bad reputation. By not letting things slip through the cracks, we have a higher percentage chance of keeping a very good reputation because we're always on top of things. Organizational skills and tools are also critical to make sure we are tracking and taking advantage of the opportunities that we're given. If we want to keep growing our business, we've got to make sure that we are not letting any of those opportunities slip through the cracks either.

Trust Is What Builds Relationships

The magic formula is trust and that's what builds relationships. Sure, we have to work hard and be really dedicated, but the smartest way to work is from a position of trust. People will trust you, even if they don't know you, if very quickly you're giving them knowledge that can help them enrich their lives.

It's very important of course that your referral sources pre-sell you as the expert. You need to have that conversation with them, letting them know where your expertise is and how you go beyond just processing a mortgage. Even if it were a cold introduction, you should begin by finding out what's important to the customer and educate them on how to tailor a mortgage that will take into consideration all of the points discussed earlier. Once you provide wisdom and insight that the customer really doesn't expect when seeking a mortgage, they will start to think, "I trust this person because it's clear this is not a job, it's a career for them." This is a way to start to earn trust, because the next thing that comes out of your mouth is going to be viewed with a lot more appreciation and respect. If we continue along that path, it's not going to take too long before the customer feels trusting and confident enough for you to become the one that handles their mortgage transaction.

Increase Your "Batting Average"

Do what you need to do to increase your batting average, and that typically means getting better every single day. I like to use the analogy of a baseball batting average. Every time you speak to a potential referral source or a potential client, that's an "at bat." How many of those are you converting into either applications or referrals? If you're like most originators, it's only one or two out of ten. Without exhausting more resources, with the same amount of incoming leads, what would happen to your business if you were able to convert five, six, seven or even eight of those? The more articulate and professional you are and the more expertise that you show on that initial conversation where you truly add value, instead of just providing information, the higher your batting average will be and the more rapidly your career will escalate.

While your competitors are closing one out of ten, you're closing six out of ten. You don't need as many leads as they do. Even if you have fewer leads, you can make more money than them and grow much more rapidly because you're closing a much higher percentage of those leads that you've got.

Don't your customers deserve the very best? That comes from giving your customers the best experience, and having the best knowledge base. Invest in yourself and into your future. This means not just investing money, but also time so that you can be smarter and better than your competition. When you get on the phone with that next customer, you have something of value to give them. It's not a magic formula; it's just learning, dedication, and the time that you put in to being wiser than your competition, and having the insights to be able to make a difference in the lives of your customers.

And guess what? The one who's the best in the mortgage industry, the one who's applied themself to getting all these tools and resources and efficiencies, isn't necessarily the most expensive. Oftentimes, they're competitively priced. So why not put yourself in that position? Be the person that, if you were getting a mortgage, you'd want to work with.

About Barry Habib

Barry Habib is an American entrepreneur and frequent media resource for his mortgage and housing market insight. For the past twenty years, he has been a well-known professional speaker on the financial markets and has had a long tenure with monthly appearances for CNBC and Fox. He is the CEO of MBS Highway, a company and platform created to help interpret and forecast activity in the mortgage rate and bond markets.

Barry has owned many successful businesses that he has founded, grown and sold. These include Mortgage Market Guide, Healthcare Imaging Solutions and Certified Mortgage Associates. His mortgage sales career included being recognized for having the highest annual origination production in the United

States on two occasions. Barry has personally originated over two billion dollars in mortgage loan production over his career.

Barry is also the lead producer and managing partner for "Rock of Ages," a long running Broadway musical theatrical production which was also released as a major film starring Tom Cruise in 2012. Barry also plays the part of the record producer in the movie.

For more information about Barry Habib and MBS Highway, visit

http://www.MBSHighway.com

Twitter: @BarryHabib

MORTGAGE STORM

Vinnie Apostolico

....

Introduction

After attending college, I had a salaried job and was working 50 to 60 hours per week but got paid for 40. Many of my friends were in sales, and I saw that they made double to triple what I was making and it seemed like they had more time off. I decided that I wanted to be on a variable income, and I was looking for the right opportunity that I could be passionate about that I could fit into.

I enjoyed skiing and during the season I was a ski instructor and I lived in a ski house with some other friends. One of the guys in our ski house knew someone that was in the mortgage business. I talked to her about how the business worked and she introduced me to an office looking for another loan officer. I decided this was my chance to get into a commissioned job. I interviewed for the mortgage position and they decided to hire me. Knowing I had to have something to live on until my commissions started coming in, I cashed out my 401(k) and joined this mortgage company in 1993. At that time I had never had a mortgage and didn't really know anything about mortgages, but I jumped right in. It was a sales position and I figured, "Worst case scenario, I would at least get an education in how money and mortgage financing works."

My decision to get involved as a loan officer has really worked out well for me and I've now been in the mortgage industry for 23 years. Today, I'm a Mortgage Banker and Branch Manager for McLean Mortgage in Fairfax, Virginia, in suburban Washington, DC.

Common Obstacles for Loan Officers

You Have to Know the Product and the Process and There Is Not a Lot of Training Available

The major responsibility as a mortgage loan officer is to bring in a steady flow of applicants, thus it's really a sales position. Unlike most sales jobs, loan officers need to know how the mortgage process works. If you are in sales at a computer company, you sell the solution, but you don't have to know how to put the computer together. In the mortgage business, you actually have to know the guidelines and how to put the deal together in addition to selling and bringing business in. In that way, I think it's actually quite a unique business.

There's not much in the way of formal training in how to become a successful loan officer. The way to learn this business is by getting business and learning on the job. When you are starting out, I suggest trying to go to work for a successful, producing manager who can train you on both the selling side as well as the technical aspects of the business.

Some Loan Officers Haven't Grown Their Business Because They're not Using All Five Pillars of Business Sources

There are five pillars that support getting business referrals for mortgages:

- Real estate agents
- Business professionals—CPAs, financial planners, insurance agents, attorneys
- Referrals from current clients
- Referrals from a database of clients one has served

- Builders

Building upon all five pillars is important to your success. I've noticed that most of the time, originators don't have all those pillars or don't have them fully developed. You do need to have real estate agents, but you need to make sure that you're targeting the correct agents. It's not that hard to talk to an agent that doesn't do any business. Targeting and talking to agents that are top producers that have the ability to generate leads for you, is critical.

Business professionals are also a key. CPAs, financial planners, insurance agents, and attorneys are all good sources of referrals. Developing those relationships to the point where they want to send you their clients and also understanding their business is very important.

One of my favorite's sources is current client referral. When you're working with a client are you turning that one loan into two, or is it just one loan and then, next? I think a lot of people miss that huge opportunity. When you have someone that's working with you, they're already sold on you. You have an opportunity to turn that person, from a one-time customer into a client, which is somebody that refers you at least one other person during the transaction. I think that's a really big piece to the puzzle.

Another one is your database, the people that you've worked with in the past. Client retention is a key. Are they going to come back to you for future purchases and refinances? Are they referring their family and friends that need a loan?

Builders can also be a good source of business. If they don't have an in-house mortgage department, they will need a reliable partner to handle mortgages for their customers. Even some builders that have in-house mortgage origination may need assistance with non-standard loans or where you can provide superior service.

Value of Mentors and Coaches

If you're just starting out, I would find someone in your area that does the level of business that you aspire to do. Try to work for that originator and use him or her as your mentor. You'll learn the technical skills to handle the loans, but more importantly, you'll learn how to generate leads and how to take great care of clients. You'll understand how to take a customer, and turn them into a raving fan.

In my first financial industry job I had a mentor that taught me the importance of saving. He preached saving a third of your income. I learned a lot from him and also from reading money books. Some of my favorites were "Think and Grow Rich," "The Wealthy Barber," and "Raving Fans." Another book I like is "Rich Dad, Poor Dad." I have probably given away over 3000 copies of this book to clients because I think it provides some good lessons in family financial management.

I immersed myself in a lot of money books because in this business we really need to understand how a mortgage fits into our client's total financial plan. As mortgage professionals, we need to be able to provide credible advice and need to know if the loan structure and payment is going to be the best choice for our clients, so they can retire financially independent.

When I got into the business, I knew some real estate agents that were about 70 years old and they were so busy because they had a huge referral-based business. They said they couldn't retire because they had too much business. I wanted to figure out how I could do that quickly, say within five years. I saw other people making ten times what I was making and thought that I was at least half as smart as them. I decided to be taught by a top producer and I was going to copy what he does. When you copy in school, you get expelled. When you copy in business, if you copy someone who has a great system, you get wealthy. Starting in 1994, I hired a coach and I copied what he did.

My coach had a system for lead generation and how to take a lead and turn the lead into a prospect and then into a shopper. From there, turning the shopper into a customer and then into a client. Then turning the client into an advocate and finally into a raving fan. I learned how to adapt his systems for my business and I combined some of his systems together, adding pieces over time. He taught me how to craft a client presentation and what started out as my short 2-minute presentation grew into a 15 or 20-minute presentation.

A very important lesson I learned is that when you spend the money to hire a coach, someone who is a very high performer and producer, you need to listen to your coach and do what the coach says. I saw many people struggle with implementation and thus their businesses didn't grow and it was always because they didn't do exactly as the coach suggested. They would go off and change things, like the words of a script or a letter. Sometimes the letter my coach was using looked like it was written by a fourth grader, but it worked. I'd copy it and it looked like a kid wrote it, but after sending it out, the phone rang off the hook. When someone who is extremely successful is telling you how to do something to emulate his success, follow exactly what you are told. I was really good at copying highly successful people that had great lives. That's what I wanted. I think you should also ask to be held accountable. If you have structure in the mortgage business, and are willing to put in the time initially, you can definitely become a master of your craft.

Keys to Success As a Mortgage Originator

Block Out Time to Do Lead Generation Before Handling Busy Work or Regular Work

Loan officers need to look at where their business is currently coming from. Many times they will say that they are too busy and their business just goes up and down. What's really the most critical thing in your business is to time-block for the activity of generating leads. After you do your lead generation activities, you fit in all the other things you have to do. More often than not, I have found that people do it the opposite way—they do the busy work, and then they try to fit in their main job, which is lead generation. When you schedule lead generation first and then fit in the rest of getting your loans done, you can start growing your business to the next level.

Sales is a contact sport. People work with people they like and trust. You've got to be out in the field, be visible and get face-to-face with people. Get to know them, so they like you and refer you. A lot of people really don't want to go out and do the work that's necessary to get there. When someone says they do, then we really want to go over their schedule and just make sure that they're doing a certain number of activities face-to-face, with their best potential referral sources. This way they can get leads and have a good, solid business.

Evidence of Success

I have a strategy that I feel is like cheating. We send out an "evidence of success" postcard to our client database that tells an interesting story of how I helped a family last month, either purchasing or refinancing. It's a transactional story, but the power is when you touch on the emotions and people can relate to it. They love it, and that's how I stay in touch with them and the phone rings off the hook with new referrals. The key is to not make it look like an ad, because then it will just get thrown away.

If you send something out that looks like a newspaper article and it looks newsworthy with a headline, it grabs their attention. Having an effective headline is really 85% of your ad. This is a great way to stay in touch with clients, providing valuable information that they want to hear about. It's been very powerful, and the client retention is huge. A lot of people are more concerned with getting new clients. If you don't retain the ones you already have, you have a big hole in your bucket and they keep dripping out.

Measure Against a Baseline

If you're a sprinter, your goal is to improve your time. If you're at a shooting range, the object is first, to hit the target, and then to hit the bull's eye. If I'm working out at the gym and I want to lose weight, I've got to measure myself. I got to step on the scale and see where I'm at. You have to look at where your baseline is. So the key to business is to increase your baseline and lower your variance. Take a look at where you're getting your business from, how you are doing it, and what changes need to be made. Most of the time it's not a huge modification that is needed to improve.

Earlier I mentioned the five key pillars that are the most common sources of mortgage business. These are real estate agents; business professionals like CPAs, financial planners, insurance agents, and attorneys; referrals from current clients; retention of your clients and referrals from clients; and builders. Most of us need to be generating business from all of the pillars to be successful. Measure your sources of business among these pillars and figure out what you need to do to increase business from each one of them.

I'm mentoring a Peak Producer class with a national coaching organization. The main topic is lead generation and we go over our students' activities to generate business. We really work on their leads, their lead tracker and pay log. We make sure they're generating enough leads and see where their business is coming from. Is it from agent or builder business? Is it refinance business? Is it their database? Is it personal friends? We make sure they have a business that is built on several pillars. Then we look at their conversion percentage, making sure they know their numbers.

Once we know what someone's business plan is, we can back the numbers up all the way. What agents are they targeting and what builders or financial planners and other business professionals are they reaching? How many leads do they need to generate per month from each one of those areas? We help them develop a plan on what they are going to do to generate the kind of business they want.

Develop Your Loyalty Ladder

When I first got into the business I noticed that most loan officers got a prospect and they move the prospect along to become a customer, someone they helped get a loan. After the loan was closed, the relationship was over. They got a one-time customer and the loan officer moved on, went back and reinvested to get another prospect. My policy is quite different; it's to be the lender-for-life of every one of my customers. As I move from the initial contact through the transaction and beyond, my objective is to move the customer up what I call the "Loyalty Ladder." I do this so they will come back to work with me again when they need another mortgage, and more importantly, to refer business to me during the process and well beyond the initial loan closing. My goal is to be their lender-for-life.

Remember the story earlier where I saw the 70-year-old agents that have too much business to retire? They have basically done the same thing and they are just serving their book of past clients and their referrals. You're always still out there selling but it's a lot more fun when your clients just continue to come back to you, and they refer you. Those kinds of referrals are like gold. When you have great referrals, they call you and request an appointment. It's a big difference from the call you get from a person that tells you he's calling three different lenders to find the one with the lowest rate.

My definition of the Loyalty Ladder is moving people along from the first contact where they are a prospect, to a customer who gets a loan through us, to a client, which we define as someone that refers us one person or comes back to us again for another loan—a repeat customer. The next level is an advocate that refers us two people and the top of the ladder is a raving fan that has referred three or more to us. Our job is to make every step of working with us a delightful experience for those we serve, and move them up the ladder.

When I first talk with a client I go over how our process works and the special service level they will be receiving. I'll tell them that most people in our business are spending time out of the office prospecting and cold calling, looking for business. I also tell them that my team and I will be here, making sure we're handling their loan and doing a great job for them and the last thing I want to do is not have my team here when they need to talk with us. I'll let them know that I'd rather take great care of my clients that know me, and that were referred to me, and that we'll take great care of them. I tell them that my team and I are going to work on their loan, and make sure that we have everything handled. Then I say, "If we do a great job for you, and you feel we have your back, then when you run into people that are thinking of buying or financing a home, please pass on my name and number, so I can help them too. Is that fair?" We generally get their agreement.

We let them know it's really their obligation, if they truly care about people they know, to make sure they get a loan officer like myself, to make sure that they're getting the best advice, and really are taken care of. We let them know that our mission is to provide their family, friends and work associates the same level of service we extend to great clients like them. We let them know that during this period of time until they celebrate the closing, they're going to run into people that are thinking of buying or financing because their "antenna" is up. During the financing process and until about 30 days after settlement our clients have the highest chance of referring us.

You've got to clearly articulate to them how you work, what's important to you, and the importance of referrals to you. The majority of people are referred to us by an agent or another client, so the next thing we do is discuss who referred them. We ask them how they know the person referring them and what they said about us. Usually, we hear something like, "Vinnie's going to take great care of you. He was awesome when he helped me." They're just basically repeating back to me that I'm going to do a great job for them. Then I tell them my relationship with the referral source and that because of that relationship I will set aside time to meet with them. I call this the "Triangle of Trust."

We let clients know that we're going to give them update calls every week on Tuesdays. If our client is calling us and asking about their loan status, we haven't done a good job. We proactively call them, so they know what's going on all the way through the process.

Once a customer makes an application with us, they have a property under contract, and we have ordered the appraisal, we also order a tin of brownies sent to their home or office, as an application gift. What we do the whole time is build a relationship. Through our actions and the updates that we provide, our goal is to take them from a one-time customer to at least a client where they refer us somebody before they go to settlement.

I also have a client care coordinator, and the whole job is to nurture lifetime relationships with our clients. My job as a mortgage originator is to find out, first of all, who are my raving fans that I currently have in my database. Then, give them the attention, because you treat them differently than a one-time customer. We stay in contact with all our clients with personal notes and email. We also conduct periodic wealth workshops and do a big party every year to say thank you.

At the end of the day, my goal really isn't just to give clients a loan. It's to improve their lives in the area of finance. I believe most financial institutions don't believe their job is to educate clients on how money works. My job is to make sure that they understand the best financing option for them and their family. Liability management and proper debt management is critical to wealth.

About Vinnie Apostolico

With twenty-three years' experience in the mortgage industry, Vinnie Apostolico is the Branch Manager for McLean Mortgage in Fairfax, Virginia. He originates mortgages in the metropolitan Washington DC area (Virginia, Maryland and DC).

Vinnie has built his business upon referrals from the many gratified customers which he has had the pleasure of serving throughout his career. It is his desire to become the Lender for Life for each of his clients on the road to achieving financial, security and community aspirations.

For more information about Vinnie Apostolico, visit

http://www.McLeanMortgageDoctor.com

Douglas Bateman

Introduction

I got into the mortgage business completely by accident over 25 years ago. I was working for a company in another industry and the owner there had acquired a mortgage brokerage business. When he bought it, everybody that was already there left and went their separate ways. He asked me if I wanted to be the manager at the mortgage company, even though I didn't know anything about mortgages at the time. I decided to give it a shot and taught myself, reading the manuals and going through the old loan files that were in the office. This is not the easiest way in getting your start as an originator, but I was able to figure it out over time and built a successful business. I attribute my success to being indoctrinated in this fashion as it forced me to become an expert on guidelines and operations in addition to merely originating.

I'm affiliated with Gold Financial where I am a loan officer and Branch Vice President in Grapevine, Texas in the Dallas/Fort Worth area. I originate loans throughout the Dallas/Fort Worth area and beyond in other parts of Texas and am the Top Producer in the entire company.

Common Obstacles for Loan Officers

It's Difficult Getting People to Trust You When You're Just Starting Out

A challenge for new loan officers is gaining the trust of prospective clients or referral partners when they are just starting out. Someone just getting into the industry doesn't have all the knowledge on the requirements to get loans approved and they could actually harm clients due to lack of complete knowledge. One approach is to focus initially on refinances while learning the business. In this way a new loan officer is helping people that are already in their house and won't cause a major disruption if a mistake is made on a home purchase transaction, harming the client.

There Is Not a Lot of Formalized Training, So It's Learning on the Job

Top producing mortgage originators make incredible incomes so there are obviously a lot of people interested in being an originator. The problem is it's not something you learn in college or in some other formalized training. Sadly the mortgage industry still seems to operate under the method of throw it against the wall and see what sticks. It's really difficult to enter the industry as a loan originator on your own because you really aren't going to know how to qualify borrowers or how to shepherd your borrowers through the loan process. I learned this the hard way, on my own, because when I took over as the manager of a mortgage company, I had to learn everything by myself. Believe me, this is not the right way to do it.

They're Not Doing Enough Sales Activities

There are a lot of experienced originators that have the potential. They are willing to work, they actually have a working knowledge of the guidelines, but they're stuck at a mediocre level. Most of the time, it's the sales side and they are not utilizing the assets they already have. Everyone hates cold calling, but you need to do something to be meeting more people and ramping up your volume. As a far superior alternative to cold calling, leverage the relationships you do have. Ask the agents you do business with for help, even if you only have one or two. Take them to lunch or happy hour and ask them to invite 3 high producing, like-minded agents from their offices with them. This could also be a meet-and-greet. Have them introduce you around. This is just one example of a way to leverage the relationships you already have.

Keys to Success As a Mortgage Originator

If You're Just Getting Started, Learn the Business Under a Top Producing Loan Officer

The best place to start, if you're newer or just haven't done a lot of business, is go to work for a top producing loan officer. You've got to suck up your pride and probably make less money for a while, but you'll get to experience a lot of different loan scenarios, while you're assisting. You need to work with someone who's doing at least fifteen closings a month. That way you are probably going to be getting exposure to sixty leads and applicants per month. That's the best way to rapidly grow your knowledge and get exposure to different client situations and loan products.

You also need to get as much education as you can. There really isn't much formal training relating to mortgages, but Fannie Mae and Freddie Mac have manuals and webinars on just about everything relating to guidelines and qualifying. Study the FHA and USDA manuals and the VA handbook. The information is all there, and these days there are regulations for many specific situations. Read these manuals from cover to cover and master them. The reality is that without learning all of the guidelines and regulations, you're providing little value to your clients. You're either going to be able to take care of your clients properly, which will grow you into a Top Producer, or you're going to be doing things in a shoddy makeshift fashion and remain one of the herd.

There are many mortgage products out there, but start with what I call the "meat and potatoes," government and conforming loans. These are products that you can master and even be become better than everyone else in your market with these standard products. These are going to be Fannie Mae, Freddie Mac, FHA, VA, USDA. You can shine with these loans and not miss a closing date. You really don't have any business doing Jumbos and non-conforming products until you have mastered the basics, which cover over 75% of all lending in most markets anyway. And then, through experience and training, you'll learn all the little variances, all the different ways to get a loan approved, and how to help a buyer make the best decision for their individual financial situation and goals.

While working under a top producer you need to start developing some partner relationships, generally with real estate agents and you'll probably be responsible for the relationships you develop. Although many salespeople don't like to do it, at this stage you'll be cold calling until you are able to develop enough high producing referral partners to build your own business. Embrace this; you could be digging ditches instead after all.

Organize Every Day to Make Sure You Are Prioritizing Time to Work on Getting New Leads First

This is a sales business and time in every day should be prioritized for working on generation of new leads. You should do that first, and then work on problems. Some people think you should work on problems first to get them over with, but you don't want to get your energy levels down before you start calling your leads. You must be energized and positive when you call new clients. Prioritize everything else in the morning as an A, B or a C. An "A" needs to be done in the next two hours. A "B" needs to be done today. A "C" can be assigned to a different completion date. That way you can always keep on top of all your important work.

Build Up Your Network of People That Are Going to Be Feeding You Clients Year-after-year

Attracting enough agents and other referral partners is just "Sales 101." You have no alternative but to make a lot of calls and try to meet as many people as possible—people that will become your best referral sources over time. You've got to start small and you've got to start hard. You really are going to need 15 good sources. "Good" means 12 closings per year from that source. Fifteen is a manageable number to stay in frequent contact with; you can't be calling on 100 people once your business is established. I call my top 15 referral sources my Channel Accounts and each one is a separate channel of business.

You really need to consider what agents to talk with when you are building your business. You'll find it is real easy to talk to a lot of agents, but most of the agents that want and have time to talk with a loan officer probably don't have any business, so you'd be wasting your time. You have to get strategic and creative to get to talk with the best agents. If you walk into a real estate office, there generally is a board somewhere with the top ten agents listed. Those are the people you want to talk to. From there, it's simple. If you can find the agents in the office go talk to them. If they are not in, try to talk with them on the phone. Say something like, "Hey I saw you're number 2 on the list! How do you do that? I've talked to eight agents today and they whine that they don't have enough business and you're overflowing with it. What makes you so great?" Then just shut up because they'll talk for an hour and everybody knows, the more you let somebody talk, the more they like you!

It's really not that hard to talk to the top ten agents in an office, but the biggest common problem people have is that they're afraid to go talk to them. It's kind of like guys are afraid to ask a pretty girl out. We wonder, "Why would they want to talk to me?" The thing is, if you talk to enough people, one of them is having a bad day. Maybe their regular mortgage partner's last three deals have gone poorly and, especially in this climate with all the regulatory changes, they're bound to have something going on that they don't like. Even if the other loan officer's doing it 100% perfect and they're just not used to the new process, or whatever it is, they're not happy that day. Maybe their guy's in Florida with his kids for the weekend; maybe he just didn't answer his phone, and you're there, and they have someone that needs help right now. Just by being the one that's available can generate business, better to be lucky than good on occasion.

We've all done the coaching about how to set up teams and limit our hours. But if you're newer in the business or don't have enough business, you need to be the one who's available Sunday night at 7 and answers the phone. You've got to start the relationship somewhere. Until they know you and they trust that you're going to get the loan handled, they're not waiting on you to get back to them. It's a different story if you have many years working with an agent. You need to learn to pick your spots and being the person available is one area where you can shine.

We have a loan originator in my office and business was lagging, because one of her best agents left the business and another one was doing poorly. She just sent out an email blast to her agent database, which basically said, "Hi, I answer my phone nights and weekends." You wouldn't believe how many people called and she had nine phone calls the first two days that were all around 8 o'clock at night and the people on the other end just said, "I wanted to see if you really answered your phone." Sometimes it's better to be available than to be good.

To me, the old fashioned methods still work the best; go out and meet people. There are a lot of networking opportunities in organizations related to real estate like Realtors® associations, builders associations and similar groups. There generally aren't that many meetings to attend, but it's a good way to meet people. Generally the biggest mortgage producers aren't going to be there, because they're too busy, so you may not have too much competition at the meetings. Email blasts can work, and that's the big reason to sign up for these organizations—to get the email list.

The important thing to do when you meet people, instead of telling them how wonderful you are, is to make a rule that, unless specific questions are asked, you don't really need to talk about yourself. Spend the first conversation with a person finding out what that agent does. Do they sell $80,000 houses or $300,000 houses? You're not going to be making money with someone selling $80,000 houses. Then on the flip side, I don't want someone who does all super jumbos. It's very hard to compete with the investment brokerages on those clients. In addition, those types of loans do not have such set guidelines like agency products, so it makes it much more likely to upset relationships with that being the case.

Work With the Listing Agent

The biggest piece of business that originators typically miss is working with the listing agent. Most originators amazingly don't want to talk to the seller's agent; to me, they're soon to be your best new agent. Many originators complain about having to speak to the listing agent. I believe that's because they must not being doing their jobs and they're afraid the listing agent will catch them on this. I always tell my clients right up front that I'm going to talk to the listing agent as well as their agent because we all have to work together to get things done properly. To me a listing agent is the best person in the world. That's an agent that's using me already, even though they didn't pick me; the buyer's agent did. But, by the end of the process they should want to use me in the future because I did such a great job with the transaction and kept them informed. Most originators miss this point and it's amazing how much quicker your business grows if you impress the listing agents. You just might get some of your best long-term referral partners this way.

Find Ways to Specialize and You May Be Able to Capture a Niche

Try to find a way to have a specialty where you can focus and be the trusted expert. As an example, I specialize in working with builders. I love working with agents and do a lot of business with the agents, but I've always done real well also with builders. The real big builders all have their own in-house mortgage companies and their management gets really rough about their agents not using their in-house originators. So when you go to these builders that have mortgage companies, you have to realize you're not going to get all their business; you're going to get their hard deals and that's okay. That's a good way to get your foot in the door, because that's also a way to meet real estate agents.

You can address this directly by going in and telling them to give you whoever they're having a problem with right now. They'll appreciate the effort, even if you can't make it work out. But eventually you start getting some of the better deals, and you'll meet the agents that are on those contracts, and that gives you more business. The big part of getting to know all these people, besides the fact that they'll throw you a bone here and there, is that you will meet many agents who specialize in selling new homes.

These companies generally will provide an incentive to the buyer for using the in-house lender. What I have found is that by doing a great job with the difficult deals, the sales people get to know and trust me. They know that by working with me, the sale is going to close, so they'll push offers where they reject the incentive but ask for closing costs reduction anyway, and they get it. So there are little ways that the good sales people will get around obstacles. Importantly, the builder gets to know that your loans are going to close. You've helped them on other transactions, so they don't make it a point to make your life miserable or try to steal your business. Agents want their deals handled properly and it's another way, if you have a good reputation, to get the business even if there are some benefits for agents to work with the in-house officer. Agents, especially top agents, don't want something going wrong with their loans and they know they can trust me.

The other thing you'll find is that builder sales people go from company to company, especially as projects get completed. If you do a great job for them, they'll introduce you around at their new job. I also like to find the smaller builders, where they don't have their own mortgage company. It's like your birthday when you get one of those. Builders are very, very loyal. They want somebody they can rely on to get their loans closed. It takes a lot of work and referrals to get the attention of a builder, but if you can solidify the relationship by taking care of their clients, you will have a good business.

Treat Everyone With Professionalism and Provide a Great Experience for the Borrower

One thing I hear from a lot of loan officers is that they hate real estate agents. I have a hard time understanding this because it's like a baker hating flour. This is where your business comes from. These loan officers will treat agents horribly. They behave as if they are entitled to the agents business and just complain about what the agent asks them to do. These people are your friends. These are the people you need to be hanging out with. You need to treat them with professionalism. Just common courtesy goes a long way, and it's amazing how little of that people get. They don't return phone calls; they don't return your emails; they don't answer questions properly. This also applies to our clients. We're not doing our clients a favor; they are paying us. If you look at the life's top ten stressors, buying a home is one step behind death of a relative. That's horrible; it should be a fun, exciting time in their lives.

We need to professionally pre-quality our clients. I see too many loan officers that just ask what a client's income is and provide a pre-qualification. They send the client out shopping for a house but have not really looked at all of the documents—the pay stubs, the bank statements, the tax returns. You really can't know the true income without looking at everything. What if they are paying child support, have IRS bills due, are taking strange deductions, or have debts not showing up on the credit report? Giving a pre-qualification without due diligence can cause lots of problems for your client. You've glanced at the credit and tell them to go out and shop for a $400,000 house. They go out sign a contract and put down thousands of earnest money. You order an appraisal and an inspection and finally your underwriter looks at the loan and determines you never should have pre-qualified it in the first place. The lack of due diligence by loan originators is frightening. Being a professional means that you find out all the issues upfront. You are providing a professional service, even if that means the client is not ready and you explain the situation right up front and provide a detailed road map for them into the future where they will be able to realize their dreams of homeownership.

I covered several keys for success in this great business. In summary, the best piece of advice for a junior person is to get on a busy and successful mortgage team, so you can learn the business. Working under a top producer exposes you to so many more loans than working with someone on the lower side of the scale. In one year you'll get exposure to as much as several years' worth of business working with an average loan officer. You may make a little bit less money initially, than working on your own up front, but to me it's an investment. You also need to expose yourself to a lot of producing agents. Once a lot of agents know you, you're really not going to need to cold call anymore.

About Douglas Bateman

Douglas Bateman has been involved in mortgage banking for over 25 years and annually ranks in the top 5% of loan originators nationwide in unit and origination volume. He is a loan officer and branch vice president for Gold Financial Services in Grapevine, Texas in the Dallas/Fort Worth area. He has been named a Five Star Mortgage Professional in 2013, 2014 and 2015 by *Texas Monthly Magazine*, where he was qualified to be among the top originators in the industry on a national level. In 2014 and 2015 Douglas also ranked #3 in Texas for his FHA volume per *Scotsman Guide's Top Originators* and has been listed in the National Register's Who's Who in Executives and Professionals

He currently hosts the weekly radio show, The Mortgage Edge, that is broadcast on 660 AM The Answer and 94.9 FM in the

DFW area, where he shares his knowledge and answers listeners questions.

For more information about Douglas Bateman, visit

http://MortgageEdge.Loans, or

https://Facebook.com/TheMortgageEdge

MORTGAGE STORM

Jason Redman

··

Introduction

The mortgage industry is a career field with a huge variety of people from all walks of life. Loan officers come from a huge variety of backgrounds and some have very compelling stories about how they ended up is this crazy career. With that being said, my story is no different. As a young man I had only one dream in life; I wanted to be a police officer to serve my community and join the military and serve my country. It just so happens that I chose both. While struggling through my first year of college I decided to join the US Air Force as a security policeman. I was trained in military law enforcement, special weapons, and ground combat. When I came back to college I stayed in the military reserves to graduate college and immediately applied at the local Sheriff's Department. While serving almost 10 years as a police officer, I worked a specialized narcotics unit, started the narcotics interdiction team, worked K-9, and was a master level SWAT and firearms instructor. I loved every minute of my service to my nation and my community. Late one night everything in my life seemed to change. My good friend and mentor in the drug interdiction field was working the same stretch of interstate that I worked and late one day he was shot and killed by a drug trafficker. It was a shock to me that one of my co-workers and a friend could be killed in an instant. Shortly after this incident I was working the interstate again and narrowly escaped being shot in the back by a drug dealer; only my dedicated K-9 partner saved my life.

That is the night I decided to walk away from my life's work, so my kids could grow up with a father. I didn't have any job lined up and no real back up plan. My whole life's purpose had been to train and learn how to be the best police officer possible. I had never thought of doing anything else. This is when I found an industry that is always hiring highly motivated people.............SALES. Soon after I entered sales, I was imagining how to become more successful in that profession, so I applied for a loan officer position at a large bank. I was quickly told during an interview with the regional manager that she had NEVER hired anyone without experience in the state of Georgia that had ever made it in the mortgage industry. She said that she doubted I would make it, but she would give me the job and would provide a desk, phone, and a computer, but I had to train myself and make my own way. Sounded perfect to me.

Before my first day at the bank I came in to complete all of the paperwork and they gave me a key to the building. On my first day I showed at 4:30 a.m. in the morning. It seemed like a good time to start the day, so I unlocked the door to the bank branch and all hell broke loose when the bank alarm and sirens went off. Seconds later, the police arrived, and when I say the police arrived, all of them arrived because the alarm showed an active alarm and the video showed a person inside the bank walking around in the dark. It was my first day, so I had no idea there were no light switches in the bank. At least they were all friends, so I wasn't held at gunpoint when my new boss arrived around 5:00 a.m. I was asked why I was there at 4:30. I said, "I thought I was starting work today; what the hours are?" She said, "The bank has an alarm; you can't go in before 9 o'clock in the morning." I wondered, "What do I do until 9 o'clock?" She just shook her head and drove off without answering me. Eventually they had to give me access to a separate entrance of the bank in the upstairs, so I didn't have to go into the main part and set the alarm off, and could still go into work so early. Interestingly, by the end of my first year at the bank, I was number one in mortgage sales for one of the largest banks on the east coast. After joining Wells Fargo in 2004, I was among the top ranked loans officers in the company for over 10 years before getting promoted to a state level position.

I've now been in the mortgage business for fifteen years and am currently the regional manager for Element Funding, responsible for all mortgage operations in Rural Georgia and the Carolinas.

Common Obstacles for Loan Officers

There Generally Is No Established Training and Little in the Way of Set Procedures

The mortgage field is a very unique career and it's highly competitive. While the earning potential can be very high, the range of pay between loan officers seems to be one of the widest gaps in the sales industry. Some loan officers make an income that is just above the poverty line and some make an income that is in the top 1% in the nation. But the problem is there are generally few documented procedures or formal training on how to do your job and do it well.

Sure, there are plenty of regulatory guidelines about who can get a mortgage and how they can get one, but generally no one is telling you or showing you how to do your job, how to source and generate your own business. Even in the most menial sales jobs in America, there is normally a step-by-step sales process. A big obstacle to most loan officers is just not knowing where to start.

When people without a sales or financial background start out as a loan officer, they have to discover a way to make the business work. Most of the time they model what they see others doing and just figure out a way to be perfectly average. That means a huge percentage of the loan officers are all basically average and average production sets the tone for what's normal. If you work for a typical company, you just go ask the person that sits next to you. The reality is you don't get an answer, because there is no measurement for what "Great" looks like. What loan officers need to learn is how to sell themselves? Knowing how to prospect and follow up with customers and clients is a rare skill these days. Once they learn this, they have to learn how to execute their sales plan every single day and be consistent. Unfortunately most loan officers have to find this training or figure it out with trial and error. That trial and error is like an income roller coaster and learning by making mistakes is a costly education that most people don't survive.

Not Recognizing That You Can Actually Be a Lot Better

Many experienced loan officers that have achieved a relatively good level of success have a challenge and that's accepting that they actually could be much better. They think that with their five or ten years of experience, and being number one in their office, making a reasonable amount of money, they can relax and be complacent.

Typically loan officers are not comparing themselves to the best in the industry and they're really capable of two or three times the business and therefore earnings, maybe more. They just need to accept that they could be better, and they could be better by focusing on the right things. The right things are prospecting, regimented follow up, and selling yourself in a way that makes you different. Loans officers that have had any amount of brief success fall directly into the habit of just responding to calls from whatever customers may need a loan this month. We have to continually build our sales value. If I asked most loan officers today to name three things they do CONSISTENTLY to get new business and tell me how long they have been doing these things, what we would find is that a huge percentage of people in this industry are doing nothing to do more business.

Too Many Loan Officers Think This Is a Reactive Business and Don't Know What to Say When Talking With Prospective Referral Sources

Another pretty common issue is that many loan officers don't know what to do before the phone rings, they just wait for it to ring, and when they do get to talk with someone, and they don't know what to say. First of all, this is not a reactive business, where you just wait for the phone to ring; you have to go out and create your own business pipeline.

When most loan officers talk with potential referral sources like real estate agents, business partners and former clients, they want to talk about their loan programs. These other people don't really want to hear what you have to say and most of your loan programs are no different than what everyone else has. They want to talk about themselves and what their needs are, and if we can just focus on our prospective partners' needs instead of our own, then we'll figure out that is what makes people call us back.

When you call people and say something like, "Hi, I'd love to come by and tell you about my company, and I could tell you about my products and programs," that sounds like you want to come talk about yourself. What a difference it makes if you call and say, "I was really wanting to add one more agent to my outgoing referral network. I've got several clients here on my desk that I need to refer out to someone and I was hoping we could meet and talk about what service level you could offer these clients. I got your name from someone that said you're one of the best in the area. I'd love to come by and see if we could partner on a couple of these referrals that I've got to send. Can you give me a call?" Your phone will ring every time.

The problem is people think we're in a reactive business, and we're not. We need to generate our own business as mortgage professionals, and we need to stop just looking for people to send us referrals. Most people think there are only one or two avenues they can get deals from, and that's agents and builders. Actually there are many places to generate your own deals, but you need to get serious about it and run your own business like it's a business. When you make a phone call, don't make it sound like you're asking for somebody to do you a favor. Generate your own networks of referrals from past clients, business associates and organizations, social media advertising and your personal sphere of influence. Then offer to refer these clients you have found to some of the top agents in your town. Stop focusing on the number of transactions you complete in a month and start focusing on the number of referrals you generate for your referral partners. You will be shocked to realize that of all the people you know, you actually generate very few referrals, because you have no sales system that works.

Value of Mentors and Coaches

I didn't have a mentor or a coach when I was starting out. I really had to figure everything out through blood, sweat, and tears and a lot of hours. Today, there are a variety of mortgage coaches that you can learn from. I'd recommend getting a good coach, but you need to talk with more than one of them to understand their methods and you should select one that meshes with your objectives and that is in alignment with where you want to get to as a loan officer.

I've come to recognize that people in this industry can dramatically and rapidly be successful if they are exposed to the best practices and they become accountable. In our company we have started an entirely new mortgage business model. When we bring new people in, we are now providing them with three months of free coaching with one of the top mortgage coaches. Our coaching provides the foundation, the systems, and the accountability. They get a tracking system for everything they do, a customer service system, a concierge-type service model for the clients, and the accountability that's so important. All of this is already built for them; all they have to do is get into the program and follow the steps. We have decided to build a model so that new loan officers get up to speed fast with technology, proficiency, and everything they need to learn to succeed.

Keys to Success As a Loan Officer

Track Everything You Are Doing and Measure the Results

Most of the time when you ask an originator where their leads and business comes from, they don't have an answer. What that means is months go by, people send those leads, but they don't know what happened to the leads. You really can't understand your business or know where your business is coming from if you aren't tracking the key metrics. How do you even know where to effectively grow your business?

Loan officers should be tracking key information like:

- Where did your leads come from?
- What was the result or disposition of each lead?
- Who was your number one referral source last month? Last year?
- How many business partners are you working with?
- How many leads did they send you?
- What percentage of your business came from agents?
- How many friends called with a referral?
- What percentage of your business came from past clients?
- What's your average loan amount?
- What's your average commission?

The reality is that almost everyone lacks these basic tracking systems so they don't know the answers. That means they don't have a system set up to track their commissions or see where their money is coming from so that they can learn and improve. Loan officers generally are not organized enough to run their business like a business, because no one's trained them and they're not disciplined enough to develop it on their own.

You need to get intentional with how you want to drive your business. Once you clearly understand where your business is coming from, you can figure out how to improve it. Accountability is also important. If you hire a coach, one of the things your coach will do is hold you accountable for actions you commit to. Nobody in this profession, or probably in any profession, wants to be accountable, especially me. I have a coach and I don't like him asking me how many leads I have, how many clients I called, did I work my database. But the interesting thing is, since I don't like having no answer to the question when asked by my coach, I go ahead and do all the things I'm supposed to do, because I know I'm accountable for it. You have to remember that to be successful in this business you have to bring your own business first. You've got at least eight or ten avenues where you can get business, instead of just calling an agent and then waiting on them to call you back. Generate your own leads. Most people don't do that because they don't know where to go to generate them, so they wait on an agent to call them.

Tracking and having accountability makes us better. If you accept that you can be better, you can be better, no matter what your production volume is today. You could be more organized; you could track things better and get better insight into where your business comes from. For loan officers that realize that, and are open to it, the sky's the limit. The good news is if you become disciplined, if you get serious, if you get super organized, it's not hard to beat all your competition.

Use Technology to Help Generate Business

Even today, there are many loan officers that don't want to use technology in their business. There are many appropriate ways to use technology, but how many of those tactics are you willing to learn and to practice? Facebook is one example. We mostly think

66

of Facebook as a personal platform to communicate with friends, but it is being used today to attract clients. Some people may say that they don't have time to get involved with Facebook, especially in their business. I know that I get two or three deals a month from Facebook. It's not about whether or not you want to be technical; it's about running a business. I'm doing it strictly to make a living, not to be popular, or to do something I enjoy.

I see the typical originator's database as the most unused client source. They are not using email blasts to the people in their database, their past clients. These are the people that have already worked with you and like you. It's not a cold call when you contact your past clients. Are you going in at least two or three times a month to market to those people? Are they hearing from you on their birthday? Do they know rates have dropped or you have some new information about ARM adjustments? You could send springtime tips and market updates. They've chosen you in the past, wouldn't they chose you again? Of course they would, or they may very well refer family, friends, and co-workers they know are looking for a new house or a mortgage.

I look at my database in the early spring and find everyone that closed a loan in the prior few months and I offer a free lawn service as an appreciation gift. I send them an email telling them to call me to schedule the lawn cutting. This just keeps me in front of as many people as possible.

Everyone that calls to say thank you, I'm going to ask them if they have a coworker or somebody they know that needs a great agent, builder, or a mortgage, and you know what? I'll get a referral. When we generate our own business that way from people that already love us, it gives us something to bring to the table when we make a call to a business partner.

Find Areas of Focus and Have Intensity to Exploit the Focus Areas

After knowing where your business is coming from, find some

areas where you can increase your business. There is a well-known theory that says that whatever you focus on, that aspect will increase. This can be applied to specific types of clients you can acquire and even on specific skills you want to develop.

Some examples of types of clients or referral partners you could pursue include:

- First-time homebuyers
- People that can be served by programs offering down payment assistance
- Clients that can take advantage of Bond programs
- Real estate agents focused on luxury properties
- Builders

You should also consider some focus on skills building. These could be polishing your sales skills, your prospecting skills, telephone skills, or creating a better presentation. If you focus on one or more of these, you will see improvement.

Now if you focus on the negative out there, like negative talk at the coffee pot, negative talk and negative thoughts are going to increase. If you focus on ten reasons why you didn't produce more last month, you're going to find ten more reasons why you didn't produce more. If instead, you focus on what it takes to get one more deal a week, you're going to get one more deal a week.

Turn What Most People Think Is a Commodity Business Into a Service-based Business Model

Most people think the mortgage business is a commodity business and everyone is competing on price. There are some small variations on the rates, but generally the rates are pretty much the same no matter who is providing the mortgage. The most successful mortgage originators turn to a service-based model where they can differentiate based on service. I've found that it isn't all about the price and the referrals come to you because business partners and clients want to do business with someone they like and receive good service from. It's not because your rate is the lowest. Referrals are the most important source of business, so you need to conduct your business in a manner that will maximize referrals.

When you provide outstanding service, you are different than almost everyone else in this business, and your clients will be much more likely to refer you. We do things at every step of the process to make getting a mortgage a great experience. It's not just processing the loan efficiently. We provide a loan approval gift, weekly communications with the client and agents, white-glove concierge service throughout the process, a free maid service and lawn cutting when the client moves in, and more. Your mortgages may be $8.00 to $10.00 per month higher, but you are likely to have much more business with the service model where you are offering an experience unlike your competitors.

When you provide this type of service, clients start telling their family and friends about how great your service is and they will remember you. You also need to use this information to let your referral partners know how to refer you. Consider how much easier the referral goes when your real estate agent partner says, "I've dealt with Jason for years; he actually is the best. Every client I send to him loves his great service. They refer their mom, their aunt, their coworkers, people at church, people at the bowling league. Everyone loves working with Jason." Your competition has all but disappeared when you receive this type of referral. I encourage you to spend time building a service model that you sell, and not just the products and programs that everyone else has. A focus on products and programs leads to everyone just wanting the cheapest and the cheapest is not always the best and there will always be someone cheaper than you. By effectively working with your partners, you'll get them referring only you instead them just giving their clients three names and saying to check with them for the lowest rate.

I've provided several keys to success in the mortgage business but probably the one key point is to set up a system of accountability. This works the best when you have a coach. Unless you know everything there is to know, and you're unbeatable, you need a coach. It doesn't matter who you are. All the great golf players have a coach. It doesn't matter how many championships they have won. As a loan officer you need somebody that's asking, "How many calls did you make last week? Are you satisfied with what you got? Oh, you didn't get any leads? Why not? Well here's why. What are you saying when you call?" Somebody who's going to break it down for you so you can get better.

Having a good coach is critical; otherwise you may just squander your time, and you'll become frustrated, and you won't develop the skills you need to be successful. You just become frustrated and stay in the business as a mediocre producer, or you leave and think it's a bad business to be in, and it's not for you. If that's the case, you just didn't give yourself a chance.

About Jason Redman

Jason Redman is the Regional Manager for Augusta, coastal Georgia and the Carolinas for Element Funding. He is also the Branch Manager for the Augusta area, where he is a specialist in military and FHA loans. Jason graduated from Augusta College with a dual major in accounting and sociology. He is a veteran of the U.S. Air Force and also served nine years at the Columbia County Sherriff's office as a narcotics investigator and member of the SWAT team.

With fourteen years of mortgage experience at Wells Fargo Home Mortgage, Jason has received awards year after year for his volume of closed loans and customer service. He has consistently been one of the top mortgage originators in the Augusta area since

71

2002, has received the monthly top producer award ninety-seven times as well as having been ranked one of the top originators in the nation from a national lender. He has been a gold/platinum award winner for the Mortgage Bankers Association for more than ten years.

For more information about Jason Redman, visit

http://www.GoRedman.com

https://www.facebook.com/Jason-Redman-Element-Funding-413445218865091

http://linkedin.com/in/GoRedman

Alex Caragiannides

....

Introduction

Like most people in this business, I never really planned to work in the mortgage industry. In 2002, I moved to San Diego from Chicago and needed to get a job. I was hired for a position as a telemarketer for a mortgage company, so I got my start dialing about 500 calls a day to homeowners. I didn't even know much about mortgages at the time, but my job was to get applications from people interested in refinancing their mortgages. After about seven or eight months, I got promoted to a junior loan officer position and started my real journey in learning the mortgage business and am now the Business Development Manager for Cross Country Mortgage in San Diego, California.

In addition to developing new business, I originate loans in the San Diego area. Throughout my career as a loan officer I've participated in coaching to sharpen my edge. I like to share my experiences and best practices with others in the industry, so I have recently co-founded BSM Academy, a training and coaching company for real estate agents and mortgage loan officers. Through BSM, I'm able to share my knowledge and experience through online training and coaching MasterMind programs.

Common Obstacles for Loan Officers

Struggling to Make Initial Contact With Prospects and Business Partners

One of the most important things to realize is that you have to self-generate your own mortgage clients. The biggest obstacle I see for loan officers, whether they are new or experienced, is in making the initial contact. No matter what you are selling, there are four parts to a sale: initial contact, building rapport, closing, and following up. It's the same in the mortgage business. You have to get out and meet people, get in front of actual potential homebuyers or current homeowners interested in refinancing, and you have to get exposure with different referral partners, specifically real estate agents and builders. Even experienced people need to concentrate every single day on client acquisition. I ask myself every day, "How can I get my name and my services in front of more people who need my services?"

Learning the Technical Aspects of the Business

Although for long-term success, 85% is related to personality, communications skills, leadership, and presentation skills, someone new to the business has to master some technical skills to get enough knowledge to get licensed. You also are going to need to know how mortgages work, understand debt-to-income ratios, qualification ratios, how to determine creditworthiness, and other details. There are some training resources made available from conventional loan sources like FHA and VA, but most loan officers learn the mechanics working under an experienced producing loan officer for a period of time.

Value of Mentors and Coaches

If I didn't have mentors and coaches in my life, I wouldn't even be in the mortgage business today. For the first four or five years of my career as a loan officer, I was working for a broker just doing refinances, not any purchase loans. I didn't know that there was another way. My first mentor taught me to run a brokerage and to always take care of customers' homes and never mess with their money. The market turned in 2007 and we had a mortgage meltdown. Everybody was affected and 2007 and 2008 was a tough time in the mortgage business. Property values dropped, interest rates went up, and few people could get a mortgage. A lot of mortgage companies went out of business and warehouse lines froze, so money wasn't available. It was an awful time. Literally 70% of the people I worked with left the business during a ten-month period. I didn't want to be like everybody else and just quit the business and go to do something else. At the time, my then-girlfriend and current wife was my business partner.

I saw an event that was scheduled not too far from where we lived. The people who were speaking and promoting the seminar had what appeared to be really good content about being successful as mortgage originators. The audience was to be made up of very successful mortgage originators, even at the same time that I was going through the struggles. They were more in the purchase transaction side, which I never knew anything about. It looked good and it felt good—the only problem was it was too expensive and we couldn't afford it. When there's a will, there's a way, so we figured a way to attend.

The event was amazing. There were a lot of great people. We heard great content and new tactics for approaching the market. Before attending the seminar, I didn't know there was another way to make it in the mortgage business and we found out that there was indeed a better way. We met people who were very successful even in the down market. The event promoters offered a coaching program for mortgage originators. It cost about $2000 per month, and with little money coming in at the time, it wasn't affordable. I said, "Well this is all I have. I'm the provider for the family. I need to figure out a way to keep us afloat. This will be my degree in mortgages." We figured out a way to do it: we put it on the credit card. That was my first experience of getting into coaching. I wasn't a huge success right off the bat. To be a really, really good when you're involved in coaching, you have to be a really humble student. You have to be very open to suggestions and ideas. You have to not ask a lot of questions—simply do everything and anything the coach tells you and learn from that. I was a little bit of the opposite. I asked too many questions. I didn't implement enough and fast enough.

During my first year of coaching, I was still struggling but finally, when I let go of everything and just said, "Okay. I'm going to let go, I'm going to give in," and just became a humble student, that's when things turned around for me. I followed my coach's advice. I learned that when somebody teaches you something, the speed of implementation is the number one determining factor of your success—or your failure.

Since that time I've had four or five coaches in my life. I like adjusting, meeting new coaches and getting different perspectives. I'm also in a mastermind group with people who aren't in the mortgage business who are helping me with social media. Right now two different people in two different industries are actually coaching me—that's how much I believe in coaching.

I like to give back as much of what I have learned to other people to help them grow in a lot of areas of their life, not just in business, but also in personal development. Overcoming obstacles is a great way of improving yourself and learning. Big breakthroughs typically happen after a breakdown. I've learned so much through my experiences, my trials, and my labors. My failures, my setbacks, and my obstacles at the time were horrible, but looking back, I can see how they were great because of what I learned and how my perspective changed. I've helped some people increase their income 300% and others increase their production while going from seventy hours a week to forty or forty-five hours a week.

Keys to Success As a Mortgage Originator

Develop the Right Mindset

A big part of success in sales, not just mortgages, is having the right mindset. The mind is one of the most important things you have. The good thing is you can feed it whatever you want, but if you don't feed it, somebody else will feed it. There's a lot of negative news and negative attitudes in the world. If you pay attention to all that, you won't be focusing on what you need to do to build your business. One of the most important things that you can do is to develop yourself in all areas of your life and have a great balance. That rolls into your professional world very well. Work on developing great purposeful thoughts, goals, visions, and plans for yourself.

I suggest all of us have our own vision statement and goals for both personal and business life. I'm big on planning. For example, I have action plans, battle plans, and strategic plans. I'm looking at my plans every day and I adjust them as needed. That's part of working on improving my business. Most people work in their business, but a lot of the magic happens when you work on your personal development as well as your business. The typical daily activities, like prospecting, are really just working in your business. When you are thinking about how to develop new marking plans or figuring out where you can get new sources of leads, you're working on the business and planning how to improve it.

I have developed a morning ritual of undisturbed time to focus and work on self-improvement. I get up very early so I can have self-time when everyone else is sleeping and I'm not going to be distracted. I like meditating right after I get up for about twenty-to-thirty minutes. Next, I read my affirmations and my goals and review my vision statement. After that I feel that I am ready to go out for a positive, successful day.

"Old School" Selling Techniques Still Work the Best and You Need to Track Everything

The starting point of the four-part sales formula is making contact and I use old school ways of doing it. I break down my activities in making contact into seven key areas and have metrics or goals for each. Number one is meeting people face-to-face. My goal is to meet fifteen people face-to-face every week. I generally do this with three people per day, but it needs to end up at fifteen by the end of the week. These contacts are applicants, potential homebuyers, business partners, real estate agents, or builders. These people are all connected to other people who can refer me business.

My next key area I call "breaking bread." Building relationships is part of building rapport, the second step in the sales process. The best way to build relationships and rapport, especially with business partners who might be referral sources, is by breaking bread. This can be as simple as having coffee or it could be a lunch, happy hour or dinner. I want to have at least five break-breads per week or one a day. The third one is phone conversation. You need to leverage the phone because you can have a lot of conversations every day. I take what I learned during my brief telemarketing career where I was making 500 calls a day and I still make a lot of calls. I try to have at least twelve phone conversations a day or at least sixty conversations a week with clients who need an application or advice on a mortgage, referral partners, business partners, past clients, and prospects. My fourth area is to send out old-fashioned, handwritten thank you cards. Almost no one does this anymore and it goes a long way to staying on top of mind. My metric on this is two cards per day or ten in a week. I use these to send a nice message to someone I just met, a new applicant for a loan, or a referral who was sent my way. I don't like the computerized cards so many people use today because they're just not as personal.

The next activity is to attend at least one networking event per week where I can meet people. This can be a typical networking event or it could be a happy hour, an open house, or a class someone is teaching that my prospects might be attending. I also teach a class once a week. It's easy to give instruction, such as purchasing tips for first-time homebuyers, VA loan eligibility for veterans, or time management for agents to different groups who need our services.

We all have own ideas about how many of each of these activities we need to do. The key is to establish metrics for yourself and make sure you are accomplishing what you set out to do. This is where tracking and measuring becomes important. I can all but guarantee that if you establish some metrics for yourself like I have done, that you won't achieve your goals unless you also track every one of these activities on a daily and weekly basis. What you measure gets done.

My seventh key area is tracking leads and deals that I get. My goal is to get at least ten leads a week, minimum, so I track that. That means referrals from past clients, referrals from agents, people who find me on my website and how many deals I get a week. These are the old school ways of doing business, but they are the basics, the foundation for any business. From there we have the new school strategies that incorporate technology, blogging, videos, emails, website, and social media. That's the new school, but I believe the foundation has to be in place first. Once the foundation is in place, you can add components with technology.

Loan officers should develop a couple of lists of people who are frequent referral sources, feeding deals in your direction. The idea is to focus communication efforts on the people on these lists. I suggest the first list include fifty top real estate agents who are likely to refer business to you. The second list should be fifty other people including past clients, business professionals, and service providers who send you business. You can have a really good year and a really good career just by taking care of those one hundred people. If each person on that list just refers to you two transactions the entire year, that's two hundred transactions—a very good year for most originators. All you have to do is take care of these people. You've got to know their birthdays and their interests. You need to check in with them, you have to call them, break bread, and send mail to them.

Get and Stay Organized

I think that being very tight with your schedule is a huge component of mortgage business success. We all have the same twenty-four hours every day but we can't manage how they fly by; we can just manage how we use the time. We need to have a really good grasp on time and how time works. What we can do is establish and manage the important activities in every day, week and year. Without a good grasp of time and important activities, we're not likely to be conscious of time and without a schedule to work from, it will be very difficult to succeed. Because of all of the daily things that arise and surprises that come up, it's very easy in the mortgage business to get off track and into a reactive mode. Once we are operating in a reactive mode, it's tough to be doing the most important activities like prospecting for new customers.

The first thing you need to do is start your weekly schedule—Sunday through Saturday—with a blank canvas. Fill in the blanks of when you are going to get up in the morning and when you are going to do your morning routine. Put it in a calendar every single day. While some people get up at 5:00 a.m. or 6:00 a.m., I get up at 4:00 a.m. The time doesn't matter; it's just that you need to have consistency and know what you're going to do when you get up. Next, schedule your personal time—time alone to improve yourself and workout or exercise time. The next phase is to schedule other personal time like family time and a date night.

Then schedule prospecting time. This is a critical part of the week and you need to block out the time on your calendar as reserved for prospecting. This includes all the sales activities I described earlier, like meeting people, breaking bread, telephone calls, networking, and others. I believe that if you are focused on success as a mortgage professional you need at least four hours a day, five days a week, devoted to prospecting. That's twenty hours per week. My personal schedule has me prospecting for five hours per day—two hours in the morning and three hours in the afternoon, or twenty-five hours in a week.

Most of us in the mortgage business don't have to punch in and out, so people tend to work whenever they want. I don't think that is a good practice and people get sloppy if they don't keep a routine. I believe you have to have structure and a schedule for when you start your day and have structure for when you end your workday.

Keep Learning and Open Your Mind to Other Ideas

I read a lot of books to expand my mind. I ask people this all the time, "Do you want a fifty-two times advantage over your competition?" Everybody I ask that question always responds with a "yes." I say, "Great, then read a book a week." The average American reads one book a year.

People look at books differently. The very wealthy people look at a book and they ask, "How can I get one great idea from this book to make my next million?" The average American looks at a book and asks, "How can I find this book cheaper on Amazon?" It's the same book but it's a different perspective depending on who is reading it. I look at every book as an opportunity to get an idea or two that I could incorporate in my life or in my business and it's drastically changed my outlook, direction, and success.

81

Be Patient

This business takes time to generate enough customers to have traction, so I advise to be patient. As a loan officer on 100% commission, you do have to be in a position financially where you can support yourself for at least six-to-nine months. Stay patient and do the right activities over and over. Focus on the activities, not the results, in the beginning. A lot of people focus on the results, but if they don't get the results quickly enough, they get very frustrated.

About Alex Caragiannides

Alex Caragiannides has been in the mortgage business for fourteen years as a loan officer and branch manager in the San Diego, California area. He has helped over 2000 families get financing for their home loans. He is a believer in old school philosophies of doing business and incorporates new school strategies to help his clients meet their goals. Alex is the Business Development Manager for Cross County Mortgage in San Diego and also originates loans throughout the San Diego area.

Alex likes to share his experiences and best practices with others in the industry, so he co-founded BSM Academy, a training and coaching company for real estate agents and mortgage loan officers. Through BSM Academy, Alex shares his knowledge and experience through online training and coaching mastermind programs.

Alex, his wife, and their three beautiful children live in San Diego. He enjoys spending time with his family and being active, enjoying the San Diego outdoors with them.

For more information about Alex Caragiannides, visit

http://www.MyLenderAlex.com

http://BSMacademy.com

http://BSMuniversity.com

http://BSMmastermindgroup.com

https://www.facebook.com/acaragiannides

https://www.instagram.com/AlexCaragiannides

Sherree Montero

....

Introduction

I started my career in real estate and mortgage lending in California about twenty years ago after selling a business that I owned. I got my real estate license and went to work for a firm that did both real estate sales and mortgage originations. As I started out, I saw that the real estate deal closings were at the mercy of the lender, so I was interested in trying to better control the entire process. I saw right away that there was an art to mortgage originations and I really wanted to learn how to structure the deals and represent the client in their best interests to obtain the right mortgage. I was only an agent for six months and then went into mortgage origination full time.

After a couple of years originating mortgages, I went to work for a prominent tax attorney in Oakland. He also had a real estate company and was a mortgage broker. I represented and managed all of his clients' real estate portfolios. A lot of his clients were big investors that had investment properties around the Bay Area. I was both the real estate agent as well as the lender on all the transactions handled with this firm and learned a lot in a few years.

I went back to full-time mortgage originations with another California-based lender. They had an opportunity in Las Vegas, so I moved here in 2001 and entered the local market at a very good time when the market was booming. I am Director and Mortgage Originator for North American Financial in Henderson, Nevada, in the Las Vegas Valley. I originate mortgages in the greater Las Vegas area and in other parts of Nevada and California.

Common Obstacles for Loan Officers

Need for Training

Due to the need to be properly trained to originate mortgages, one of the most critical decisions when starting your career in the mortgage industry is choosing the company to work for. We really don't have schools like the real estate industry has, and that's why I think it's so important that you find a company that has a comprehensive training program so you can give yourself the best chance for success. This decision can result in a very positive beginning, or it could be very detrimental to your career, so you really need to do your due diligence on the company. I suggest finding an employer who offers the best training, support, and technology platform. Technology has become more important because of the way our business has changed over recent years and because Millennials, who are driving a lot of our business, are interested in interacting using mobile technology.

The beginning of your career will be much easier by getting proper training and growing the skills you need to qualify clients. You also need to understand the loan process so you can effectively close your loans on time. The most successful originators rely on past clients and referrals to build their business so reputation and maintaining great relationships are critical. You don't want to be learning the loan process on your customers.

Not Having Effective Marketing and Systems

For the most part, being a mortgage originator is like being self-employed. You are responsible for finding clients and the money you can make is pretty much proportional to the amount of business you can do without many limitations, except the ones you put on yourself. After working as an originator for a while, a lot of us get stuck at a certain level where we just don't grow any more. With the potential being almost unlimited, we need to figure out why we have plateaued.

Much of the time the issue is that we are not keeping up on technology or other changes in the industry, not effectively marketing, and we haven't developed systems to make us more efficient. Essentially we have our own business and we need to invest in ourselves and in our business to become the best we can be. I've found one of the keys is to surround yourself with people that are more successful than you are at what you do and learn from them. This can be a top producer in your own company that is willing to share knowledge and help. Another way is to find a good coach that has great marketing programs as well as systems to make your business run smoothly.

Value of Mentors and Coaching

I started out in sales at an early age and invested in sales training, mostly through the Tom Hopkins Group. Some of the things I learned from my early training still influence me to this day. One concept is that knowledge is power. The more you know your industry, the more you know your job, the more powerful you can be in it. If you're just starting out, try to identify a mentor, someone who is a top producer and is what you aspire to, and learn from your mentor.

Although I have quite a bit of experience and have been a top producer, I have been stuck myself at times. I recently hired a mortgage coach to guide me to the next level. By getting another point of view and learning from my coach, I have been able to tighten up my internal systems, set up improved lead tracking methods, and expand my marketing outreach. Hiring a coach has been a great investment for me and in a short time he has helped me dramatically increase my business without having to work additional hours.

Keys to Success As a Mortgage Originator

Develop Your Business With Superior Service

Marketing is a critical component of your mortgage business to find new sources of referrals and clients. Marketing won't do you much good though unless you have a very good reputation. As you are establishing and growing your origination business, try to stand out from the competition with your level of service. Sometimes this is as simple as staying in touch and communicating with your client during the processing of their loan. It's a nervous time for the borrower, who has a closing deadline, and both agents don't get paid unless the mortgage closes. I've found that by providing weekly email updates to the client and the agents, most of their anxiety disappears and they don't have to wonder what is happening or have to chase me down. The agents will develop a lot of confidence in you if you provide great communications, as they may not be getting the same level of service from other lenders.

Developing consistent internal processes will help to keep all of your loans moving along, even as your business grows. Your entire process, including communication protocol, should be mapped out in a template and streamlined to make it as efficient as possible. This will produce consistent results and clean approvals on a timely basis to speed each mortgage along to the closing. Providing exceptional and consistent service is a key to building a referral-based business by exceeding expectations of your clients and real estate agents. Once you have these things in place, it really makes your marketing more effective.

Start Marketing During the Transaction

The most successful people in this industry have a business that is largely based on referrals, not just one-time clients. A powerful insight I received some time ago is that if your client refers you during the time you are doing their loan transaction, the chances go up to about 80% that they will refer you at least once in the future. What I have done is to find as many opportunities as possible to try to get referrals from my clients before the closing. Not only the borrower, but also the real estate agents on both sides of the transaction, are emotionally involved and vested during the transaction. The borrower is very excited about getting into a new house and the agents don't get paid without a closing.

The client is most excited right after their offer is accepted and right up until they move into their new house. This is also a time that they will be most aware when a friend or acquaintance mentions they are thinking about buying or selling a property. I always ask a new client to let me know if they know someone that is thinking about moving or selling their house. I also make this inquiry a few times while the loan is being processed.

Many originators never communicate with the listing agent, but as soon as there is a contract I start by introducing myself to the listing agent and send a marketing package with contact information. I also let the agent know what kind of service to expect from my team. I do this to build confidence and trust with the listing agent and they get an immediate indicator that they are not working with the typical lender. I go over the property details with the agent, inquiring if there are any issues, upgrades or improvements that will affect the appraisal or the inspection. Also, I inquire if they have valid comps. All of these things can be of assistance when we order an appraisal.

Every listing agent is a potential partner for me. By starting out immediately establishing communications and elaborating on my service model, I'm opening the door up to be able to set an appointment with them to move in the direction of working with me a lending partner. I always immediately communicate if there is a problem or if I'm rescoring a client. Everyone respects honesty and you never want to stretch a deal out and not let anyone know until it's too late, jeopardizing the deal.

Once the loan has been approved I have one of my team members go to the borrower's workplace and deliver a congratulations card with a basket of goodies, like popcorn or some other nice snacks. We leave a stack of my business cards and the referring agent's business cards and let everyone know how to contact us if they or someone they know is interested in re-financing, buying, or selling a house. Many times, just by doing this, we will immediately get some leads for our team as well as our agent partner on the deal.

I also like to use our clients' influences, like the places they work. After the closing I'll send out an employer's package introducing myself, saying that we've recently closed a loan for one of their employees and that we'd like to open up a partnership and offer discounts on closing costs and more to their employees. We also include business cards from the agent partner on the transaction. I've found this to be important and beneficial because I can show the agent that we are actively working on cross-selling both of us to the employers of our clients, and working to generate future leads for both of us.

Have a Purpose and Develop a Related Referral-based Niche

I recommend that people entering this business try to find a purpose for what they do and use their purpose as a mechanism for positioning to build a better referral-based business. Mortgage origination is a career, and it's easier and more fulfilling doing business with like-minded people who are aligned with your belief system and work ethics. Giving back to the community and helping people achieve their dream of home ownership are examples of having a purpose. I think that marketing and branding around your purpose positions yourself a step above the rest, and makes you more competitive. In this industry we are providing advice and helping our clients make the best decisions for the financial side of their lives. We do this by education and by developing their trust in us to put them into the most appropriate mortgage for their individual situation.

My purpose is derived from role models in my family and personal experiences involving community heroes. My family was large and we had a number of family members in public service as police officers and firemen as well as in the U.S. Armed Services. I will never forget how proud I was the day my cousin, who was the first person of Hawaiian decent to become a Three Star Army General and who was the deputy commanding officer of the U.S. Army Forces Command, was honored for his 38 years of service. I also remember an experience when I was nineteen and was driving home from a ski resort in a blizzard and had a really bad auto accident caused when another vehicle went out of control. My friend and I were stuck in an overturned car in a snow bank, couldn't get out, and were about to freeze. Fortunately, we were saved by a state trooper, who came by and rescued us. These experiences have motivated me to develop a purpose in helping heroes in our society.

Homes For Heroes® is a national organization that partners with the real estate and mortgage industries to give back something to the heroes in our community, like policemen, firemen, healthcare workers, teachers, active military, reserves, and veterans. It's a private sector organization giving back as a way to say, "Thank you," to these heroes and for what they do every day for us. Partnering with Homes For Heroes has become a way for me to facilitate my passion of honoring heroes that serve our community in a tangible way. By working with lenders and real estate agents participating in Homes For Heroes, the client saves with a discount on the closing cost from the lender as well as a discount credit on the real estate side.

I have found that by making Homes For Heroes my purpose, I have the doors opened to work with different spheres of influence like police departments, fire departments, hospitals, and schools. My fees are lowered by giving back and offering these benefits; however, it has been a great way to develop really great partnerships and friends in the communities I serve, and importantly has helped me develop a referral-based business. I'm continuing to give back by co-sponsoring events in the community, like golf tournaments along with a hospital and the police department, which helps me meet more people and develop additional relationships. This is all very powerful and I'm having a lot of fun being involved.

Use Co-branding to Strengthen Agent Relationships

Earlier I mentioned that when we go to the client office to deliver a gift basket, we provide our marketing materials and business cards as well as business cards from the referring real estate agent on the deal. This is a way to show our agent partners the value in working with us, as it's not just a one-way street, where the referrals are only going in only one direction.

I have a mobile phone and tablet app that features a loan payment calculator, a home affordability calculator, identifies the ideal loan type, and details the home buying process for users. My app is set up to co-brand with a number of my agent partners. The user gets to see agent and loan officer photos, profiles, and contact information. This has been another way to provide value to my real estate agent partners and is one more way to provide value and strengthen our relationship.

Market to Your Database

Clients that have worked with you in the past and have received a great experience are one of your best sources of repeat business and referrals. Unfortunately, many loan officers just go on to the next deal and don't market to past clients. As I previously discussed, if a client refers someone to you during the transaction, they're much more likely to refer you in the future. You do need to stay in front of them and you need to be organized to effectively communicate with them on a periodic basis. This becomes easy when you use a Customer Relationship Management (CRM) system.

I load each client into my CRM system and set it up with information on birthdays, anniversaries and the original referring agent. By the way, this is another co-branding tool I use, as I co-brand the messages I send along with the agent linked to the client. My CRM is set up to send automated messages to celebrate birthdays and anniversaries and I also send out information on mortgage market updates, suggestions to get together for periodic loan evaluations to see if refinancing is a good option, and to ask for referrals. Once the CRM is set up, it's easy for one of my assistants to send out a mass email with a few clicks.

About Sherree Montero

Sherree Montero began her real estate career in the San Francisco Bay Area as a Real Estate Agent and Loan Officer over 20 years ago. After two years she was hired by a prominent tax attorney as a Real Estate Asset and Portfolio Manager for his clients. In this role, she was responsible for maximizing real estate asset value through acquisition, operation, re-positioning, and disposition along with buying, selling, and financing all property types.

Sherree has been based in the Las Vegas Valley for 15 years, and became a top producer in the market shortly after arriving from Northern California. The superior level of customer service she provides sharply distinguishes her from other mortgage professionals. She is Director and Licensed Mortgage Originator for North American Financial in Henderson, Nevada.

For more information about Sherree Montero, visit

http://www.TheMortgageMaker.net

https://www.Facebook.com/SherreeTheMortgageMaker

MORTGAGE STORM

Richard Lytle

··..

Introduction

After graduating from college I started a sales career selling health and life insurance in Wilmington, North Carolina. I was learning the ropes about all the techniques and tactics required in selling and I was doing fairly well. I was also a new father at the time so it was important to me to maintain a stable income. One day I received a phone call from a good buddy of mine from college. We were just catching up, and talked about what we were doing. My friend was originating mortgages and asked if I might be interested in looking into the field. He talked about how much money he was making and I didn't really believe it was possible. After proving his earnings to me I thought I'd better take a look at getting involved with mortgages.

I decided to interview with a mortgage company and a day after being interviewed, I was offered a mortgage job in Winston-Salem, a few hours away. We decided to make the move and I got started in the mortgage industry. After working there for a year, we missed Wilmington and decided to come back. I was able to get a job back here in Wilmington handling mortgages for a bank. I've worked for some other mortgage companies and have now been with On Q Financial for about four years. With fourteen years of mortgage experience, I originate mortgage financing in the greater Wilmington area, along the southeast coast of North Carolina. The great thing about being a mortgage originator is that you have the opportunity to determine your own income, because your commissions depend on individual performance. That's what drives me and all of the top performers in this industry.

Common Obstacles for Loan Officers

Starting Out, Loan Officers Need to Develop Their Own Client and Referral Base

To have any success originating mortgages, new loan officers have to go out and find their own clients. This is not a business where you go to sit at a desk and wait for the phone to ring. The first thing that has to be done is go out and start contacting all of the people you are acquainted with and let them know what you are doing and that if they know anyone buying a house or interested in refinancing, that you are handling mortgages. Networking skills and people skills are really important in a business like this. Think about everyone you know and make a list of all the people you can contact. This can include former teachers, friends, family, business owners, and business professionals.

I believe that real estate agents are the best source of clients because almost all real estate transactions start with an agent and the agent, much of the time, refers their buyers to a mortgage company. After talking to all of the people who already know you, contacting and trying to work with agents will be a big key. The problem is that real estate agents will turn down a new mortgage officer over and over. They have a lot at stake if something happens with the mortgage on their deal, so they are very cautious in whom they work with. They're going to test you and your skills and knowledge. They're also going to test your communications capability because they recognize that is one of the most important aspects of the mortgage business. If you can't communicate, or get back to the client or agent in a timely manner, you're not going to be a good referral to send buyers to. You have to be persistent and you need to let them know that you will be available to them if they run into a snag on a deal they are working on. By being the one available, even outside of normal business hours, there will likely be some cases arise where their regular mortgage partner is on vacation or not available for some other reason. Or, maybe their mortgage partner has recently been slipping up on service and it's time to give you a try.

Some Experienced Loan Officers Get Stuck Because They Don't Know What to Do to Grow Their Business

Some experienced loan officers get stuck at a certain point and may get complacent. It may because they don't know what to do to take their business to the next level or they don't understand the amount of money top producers in this industry can make. Surround yourself with people that are doing better than you are and learn from them. Associating with people making more than you are tends to bring you up to their level. Here's a good analogy. You have a big dog, say a yellow lab. Then you bring in a puppy that grows up to be a small dog. As they spend time together the small dog starts thinking and acting like it's a lab, a big dog. Who you are associating with is going to be extremely important to the success of your career.

I suggest you seek out a top producer to work for early in your career because you can learn so much more from someone who mirrors what you want to become. If for some reason this is not possible, find top people outside your company to have personal discussions with to find out what they think are the keys to being successful and what works for them. You could also hire a coach to help you with best practices, strategies and accountability.

Value of Coaching

I had been progressing in my career as an originator and doing fairly well, but still wanted more. About five years ago I was introduced to an event, called "The Mastermind Summit," held twice a year, that brings together some of the top people in the mortgage industry in the country. I looked at the agenda for the event and it seemed like an opportunity to hear what a lot of top mortgage producers are doing to grow their businesses. I decided to attend and spent my own money to fly out to Las Vegas to experience and learn from some of the best. My vision started changing right there during the event. I learned a lot of sales tactics and other ways to grow my business during the presentations. More importantly, I met many, many other mortgage people that were making hundreds of thousands per year, some even over a million dollars per year. I had never realized how much money could be made and, a light bulb went on in my head as I thought, "Wow, I can do this, too."

I also met a number of mortgage coaches at the event and soon started working with a coach. I have learned a lot by working with coaches over the past few years, and most recently in the past year or so, I started working with one who has helped me substantially. I have learned and implemented systems to track everything I'm doing in my business including leads, conversion rates, how much I'm spending on every aspect and how much commission I am earning. I've found that tracking everything helps me learn what's working and what's not. Measuring everything then provides clarity on what to do next.

Keys to Success As a Loan Officer

Start With a Vision and Proper Mindset

Most of us hear about vision statements, but we think they mostly apply to a company or an organization. Each one of us, individually, should have our own vision statement, laying out who we are and who we want to be. Part of this is our purpose—why we are in this business and why we want to make money from our work. Once you understand your purpose and your vision for the future, it becomes much easier to think through the steps that need to be taken to achieve your vision. If your expectation is to be top producer, you need to be able to envision yourself as a top producer.

Working as an originator in the mortgage business is most importantly a sales function. Just like in any sales job you need a positive attitude and mindset that is focused on achieving your goals and winning if you want to become a top producer. There are always going to be setbacks and there's no time for making a bunch of excuses when things aren't going your way, moving into a negative mindset. In this business you have to go out and generate your own business, and this is mostly by connecting with real estate agents and other business partners that can refer business. You need to have the confidence in yourself that you can provide a value to partners and their clients because when you're out there meeting with potential partners, experienced people can tell if you are lacking confidence in yourself. If they don't see you have confidence in yourself, they won't be likely to have confidence that you can properly handle their clients.

Block Time Every Week for Prospecting Activities to Build Your Business

It's too easy to get caught up in the mortgage process and then start getting consumed by all of the distractions that are inevitably going to happen every day. No matter what level a loan offer is at, prospecting, building, and maintaining relationships is a major factor in both short-term as well as long-term success. Successful originators block out adequate time during every week to prospect and cultivate relationships. Most of us call it our "green time," which is our money time. The key point is to block this time in advance and don't let anything else take over the time that has been blocked.

Here are a few examples. Say on Mondays you decide to block out two hours for calling potential partners to set up in-person meetings later in the week. These could be meetings with agents, builders, CPAs, or financial advisors. You block the time and only do that activity during the appointed schedule. On Tuesdays, you could block time to call your pre-approvals, those clients that you've pre-approved, but that are hunting for a house. It's just touching base with them to make sure you are staying in front of them so that when they find their home and get their offer accepted, you're still the one they will be working with for the financing. Just like any other partners or referral source, you can lose that client if you don't stay in contact with them.

Time should also be blocked out every week to work your database. This is going back through your database of people you have worked with in the past, and looking for possible opportunities. This could include contacting past clients that might be good candidates for refinancing if rates have dropped as well as to see if your past clients know of anyone that may be shopping for a house that they could refer. You could also reach out to see if they can help you connect with their current employer to become a preferred lender for the employees. Let's skip to Friday. On Fridays you could block time to call the real estate agent partners that you currently work with and let them know that you'll be available over the weekend if they have a need. You also might want to inquire if they have any clients that need to get a pre-approval.

Although it is easy to put these critical activities, or other business-building activities, on your calendar, it can be difficult to follow through and actually commit the blocked time to the appointed purpose. Too many times chaos starts happening and other emergencies pop up during our day, but if we are not doing these critical activities required to grow our business, we can easily fail. You want to create good habits so you make sure that you are allocating an appropriate amount of time every week to business growth activities and stick to your schedule for these activities.

Leverage Connections with Real Estate Agents by Working with Agent Teams

Like most loan officers, quite a bit of my business is referred from real estate agents. When you target an individual agent, working alone, you're just going to get whatever that agent can refer to you. Sometimes it's hard to figure out if they're doing a lot of business, so you could be wasting time if they're not doing a reasonable volume.

Much of my success is due to targeting and then working with real estate agent teams. Over a number of years agents have banded together into teams to spread their coverage and to develop a better service model for their clients. Sometimes individuals on a team will have different specialties, like working with first time homebuyers, working with vets, or working different submarkets. Typically these agent teams are top producers, developing and closing high volumes of sales. I have found that by working with teams, my time is leveraged and I am able to get referrals from most of the team members once I get into an established relationship with the team.

Create Systems to Standardize Processes and to Efficiently Manage Time

Successful originators learn what works and then create standard procedures for all aspects of their business. Procedures need to be systemized so that important aspects that have been established will always be carried out and not forgotten. As an example, I have set up a process for what I do after meeting with a potential real estate agent partner. After my first meeting, I have several steps I follow to keep in front of the agent and to follow up after that first meeting. I send out a hand written thank you card following the meeting. Next, I want to set up another call to schedule a meeting to go over key points that were discussed in the first meeting. I like to send them a small gift like a box of popcorn to their office. The challenge is to remember to do all of these follow-up tasks in a timely manner. I have found that it is easy to automate the scheduling and reminders to do these activities. I call it a project management board. It can be a manual system, but today there are so many simple software tools that can be used to automate the scheduling of your standardized processes. Customer Relationship Management Systems, or CRM Systems, are available to handle this on your computer. There are even systems available specifically tailored for the real estate and mortgage industry.

I have also set up a standardized process for clients when they get pre-approved. I set up several routine tasks and my system tells me when to periodically contact them, send out a thank you card, send out a small pre-approval gift and ask for referrals as they are house hunting.

Create Ways to Demonstrate Expertise in the Mortgage Field

No matter what field you are in, people want to do business with the expert. As mortgage consultants we need to find ways to demonstrate our expertise, which will make us more attractive to our prospects. I have focused most of my lead sources on real estate agents so I considered how to stand out and become known as a mortgage expert in my local area among the agents. I found something that not only helps define me as an expert, but it also gets me in front of a lot of agents.

Typically, I will participate in continuing education courses with real estate schools, and teach certain aspects of mortgages. I also team up with organizations that provide specific financing programs or products. For example, I team up with North Carolina Housing Finance Agency to do seminars for realtors on down payment assistance programs that can open up access to purchasing houses to a lot more people. This is clearly a benefit to the agents as they are learning about some ways to expand their universe of possible clients. As the teacher of the classes, I can show that I am an expert and I am helping agents broaden their client base. Generally about thirty to forty agents will attend these classes, so it's another way for me to make an impression and I get to meet many new potential partners every time I teach a class. I participate in teaching these classes several times per month.

Now that I have received the benefits of being coached and have used the knowledge gained to grow my business, I like to give back to others, helping to make a positive impact in their lives. I work with a lot of agents in the area, helping them with some of the things that I've learned through being coached. I try to share with them how to become a better real estate agent, ways to approach clients, how to proactively respond to their clients and help to set goals and organize systems. This is another method to establish positioning as an expert and really helps me solidify relationships with agent-partners. Every once in a while an agent I'm not working with, who has seen me present at a course, will approach me and request coaching. When you devote some time with these agents into their development, they greatly appreciate it and much of the time it leads to business opportunities.

About Richard Lytle

Richard Lytle has been a mortgage loan officer for fourteen years, with the last eight years serving the Wilmington, North Carolina area and surrounding counties. He is a Producing Manager for On Q Financial in Wilmington. To continually educate clients, Richard has partnered with CPAs, tax accountants, real estate agents, builders, bankers, insurance agents, and even other mortgage professionals to make the process of buying a house as smooth and stress-free as possible. He is also a frequent instructor of classes for real estate agents, teaching topics about specific mortgage products and down-payment assistance programs.

Richard is a dedicated husband and father of a beautiful daughter. The importance of family drives him to help other people and their families. He is involved in the Wilmington community serving in guest services at Port City Community Church and helps raise money for the Red Cross, American Cancer Society, Make A Wish Foundation, and Muscular Dystrophy. He has also served as the President of the Wilmington Advisory Board Chapter of BNI and is involved with the "Wilmington Leadership" program organized by the Chamber of Commerce.

For more information about Richard Lytle, visit

http://WilmingtonMortgagePlanner.com

https://www.facebook.com/RichardMortgages

https://www.LinkedIn.com/in/RichardMortgages

MORTGAGE STORM

DeAnn Ellis

....

Introduction

I've been involved in the mortgage industry for eighteen years now. Right out of high school I got a job with a local community bank, initially as a teller, and then I quickly became the lead teller. Soon after I started to work there, the bank was acquired by a large national bank. The branch manager suggested that I move over to the consumer lending side, so I started doing car loans, second mortgages, and home equity lines of credit. Not long after I transitioned into that position, I became a regional top performer, out producing people that had been there 20-25 years. I moved up the ladder very quickly after that.

One of my customers was a branch manager of a mortgage company and she liked working with me and inquired if I would be interested in working at her company. I had a strong desire to work with mortgages but the 100% commission scared me a bit and wasn't sure if I wanted to get into something risky without a stable income. Nevertheless, I ended up taking the leap and accepting the position and a lot of my clients followed me from the bank. My career in the mortgage industry blossomed from there.

Today, I'm a Senior Loan Officer for Element Funding with an office in Covington, Georgia. My team and I service all of Georgia.

Common Obstacles for Loan Officers

Fear of Going Out and Talking with People

There are some obstacles that new originators must overcome in order to be successful in this industry. For a lot of people, fear is a big block to their success. A lot of new mortgage originators don't know what to do to go out and get business. Or, they are afraid to go out and talk to new people and introduce themselves, in the context of the work they do in the mortgage industry. This is not a business where you sit at your desk and wait for someone to call or to come into the branch office. It's about networking and proving yourself. You have to actually go out, talk to real estate agents and other professionals. I suggest getting involved in Chamber of Commerce and Realtor® Board events and other networking groups to meet as many professional people as possible. Keep in mind that when you are new, it can be difficult to convince agents to send you a deal. When they do, you have to do a great job.

When I was building my business, meeting face-to-face with real estate agents and other professionals was almost all that I did. I would work on my loans at night and in the morning, and I would take off around 10:00 a.m., and I would drive to agents' and builders' offices. I would also attend social events, Chamber of Commerce, and business networking events. I would come back to the office around 3:00 p.m., and start working on my loans again. You have to continually focus on prospecting, or you will never make it in this industry. If you are out of sight, you're out of mind.

Lack of Knowledge

Lack of knowledge is another obstacle for new loan officers. Some people want to jump in fast without the knowledge and don't know how to put their clients into the right loan program. If you make a wrong decision on a mortgage file, it affects a lot of people—the homebuyer, the agents on both sides of the transaction, and the seller. The mortgage business is very complex. You have to be knowledgeable and be able to close on time. The best way to start is to work as an assistant to an experienced loan officer, so that you can be mentored and learn the business under their guidance. This may seem like a slower path to the money, but for the medium to long term you are much more likely to be successful if you take it a little slower and learn how to work in this industry in the correct manner.

They Have Not Developed a Team and Are Resistant to Delegating Tasks

When you're starting out, you have to do everything from beginning to end—every task is yours to complete. That's what makes you a good originator because you learn the entire process. When I first started out in the industry, I did not have an assistant as I didn't have the volume to justify one. At some point as your business is growing you hit a wall. As a loan officer becomes successful, all of their time capacity is consumed and it is difficult to grow the business further. You either have to ramp down prospecting, which clearly will limit your ability to grow further or you won't be able to handle all of the loan files. Many find it difficult to break through this wall and move to the next level.

Once you get to where you can't handle everything, you need to have some additional resources and bring somebody else in to help handle the details of the transactions. You also need have the confidence to delegate to your team, as this is another frequent sticking point for some people. The way to develop that kind of confidence is to thoroughly train your team members with the knowledge that you possess and in all of your procedures so they will handle the tasks the way you handle them. If you don't delegate and try to control everything, it will be difficult to expand the volume of business that you do.

Value of Mentors and Coaches

The branch manager that hired me in my first mortgage job was very successful and she mentored me, showing me how to go out and get business, how to manually qualify borrowers, and all the core things you have to do to be successful. At a very young age, I realized how strong your work ethic has to be, how much you have to work.

More recently, I have had a coach to help me organize, track and set up systems. My business had already been successful; however, by using my coach's systems, I have been able to streamline the business. I have a large team and it was hard to get my hands around everything, so coaching has helped me organize my business. Working with my coach, I set up a lead tracking system, so I now know exactly where my leads are coming from and I can see exactly who to reach out to. We also set up a system that keeps track of the status of loans going through the process and that automatically sends me text messages with status updates.

I have had a team helping me over the past sixteen years and have been coaching each new member as my team has expanded. It's very fulfilling to me to see people that I have brought in and coached become very successful. One of my loan officers has been with me for a few years now and is going out finding her own business and originating mortgages. I gave her the confidence and the knowledge that she needed to develop her own business and she goes out and meets with the agents and other referral sources. She went from being a secretary at a different company and now makes really good money as a loan officer. I originally met her as my client helping her with her mortgage. After handling her mortgage, she told me, "I want more out of life. I would love to do what you do. How can I learn the mortgage business?" So, I literally sat down and went over the industry with her, decided to hire her as an assistant, and trained her to be a very effective and successful loan officer.

Keys to Success As a Mortgage Originator

You Need to Be Willing to Work Hard and Be Passionate About What You Do

First of all, you're going to have to be extremely dedicated. Know that your job affects people's lives and you have to be passionate about it. You have to want to help people; it really can't be just about the money. I'm passionate about helping people, and want to literally eat, breathe, and sleep the mortgage industry. If you don't have a similar passion, it's probably not for you. You can get by. You can make a reasonable income, but in order to make several hundred thousand dollars a year, you have to make sure that it's your passion and that you're willing to go over and beyond the call of duty.

You've got to be willing to work hard and pretty much be available all the time. On Saturday, if you're at the mall and an agent calls, you have to answer your phone. I do a lot of loans, but at the end of the day I get a lot of fulfillment when I have a client call me and say, "Thank you so much! Without you, we never would have been able to become a homeowner." That is what drives me.

There's a lot of flexibility with work hours and place, but you're not likely to succeed unless you develop a structure to your work. You can work from your house, your office, or even a hotel room if you are traveling. As long as you have a computer and a phone you will be able to work. I think with the flexibility a lot of loan officers lose sight of the need to maintain structure in work habits. If I work from my house, I'm not washing clothes or watching TV, I'm focused on my job. I think a lot of loan officers because we have such leniency in our industry, lose sight of what's important. This is a job; it needs to be structured in order to be successful.

Pick a Market and Saturate It

Second, you need to know your market. I suggest that while you're building your business, that you concentrate on a reasonable size specific geographic area. You can't be effective trying to serve a very large area. Pick your area, and then saturate it. Your objective is to become known by as many real estate agents in your target area as possible and also to network with business people in your area. You won't be able to capture all of the agents as referral partners, but if you can develop a solid relationship with at least fifteen top producers, you can have a good business.

I've found some good places to network are at the Board of Realtors® groups as well as the Chamber of Commerce. I actually am a member of two of the local realtor boards as well as the local chamber. I've been active in these organizations and by being an active member, I have been elected to leadership positions. The leaders have a lot of exposure and by being involved as a leader my name is very visible to the full membership, another way of attracting notice and attention.

I also meet face-to-face with individual real estate agents and other professionals that may be able to refer business. When I visit real estate agents at their offices I do some things to leverage the meeting. I like to bring in a box of gourmet popcorn as a gift to the office. I also bring along flyers and business cards. I've found everyone in the office wants to sample the popcorn and wonders where it came from. My flyers and business cards are there next to the popcorn and this is just another way to be noticed. I learned to do this many years ago and I'm amazed that almost no one else does it.

We market extensively to our database in the area. I gather business cards from people I meet at networking events and meetings and when I get back to the office my assistant logs them all into our database. We maintain frequent communications with the people in our database including flyers and newsletters aimed at real estate agents. My office also hosts a monthly happy hour for agents in the area. This has been really effective in getting the agents to know our team. By hosting our own happy hours, we are the face of the events and they are a great way to build and maintain our relationships.

Communication Is Critical

Good communications starts with the initial client contact. I attribute a lot of my success to the way that I handle my clients from start to finish. For example, recent trends are to automate the application process so loan officers don't have to spend time taking an application. I have taken the opposite approach, preferring to have my staff taking the application from the client either in person or over the phone, unless the client requests to apply online. We like to establish a relationship with them right from the beginning. Buying a home and getting a mortgage is a scary process, especially for first-time homebuyers. I believe that if you establish a personal relationship while you're getting all of their personal information you develop rapport as a trusted advisor. Even if a client decides to apply online we always call and conduct an interview over the phone, just to make sure all the information we have is accurate.

There are pros and cons to the old fashioned method instead of just having everyone apply online. When you break down the time it takes to speak with a client, it does take longer, but I also think I've captured a lot of business using the personal approach.

When we qualify borrowers, we educate them on the entire process. The mortgage industry has changed so much in recent years—even the closings have changed. We send each client an email detailing the do's and don'ts. We send a list of items that we need, and when the borrowers come in, especially first-time homebuyers, we make sure that they completely understand the process. There are no stupid questions. They are fully educated when they leave our office and we want to ensure that they feel comfortable with the transaction.

Communications with your borrowers and the agents on the transaction are critical as the loan is progressing toward the closing. Remember that purchasing a home is one of the more stressful experiences in life. Proper handling of the transaction is also critical for the agents who don't get paid unless the loan closes on time. Some loan officers aren't very consistent with their communications, not answering the phone or not even returning calls in a timely manner. This only heightens the stress for the borrowers and agents, especially when they are wondering about the status of the loan file. I've actually developed a more proactive approach, where my team communicates a status update on the same day every week while the loan is in process. We provide the status update by email to the borrower as well as the buyer's agent and the listing agent so they don't even need to call us.

This brings up another great point. Most loan officers don't even communicate with the listing agent. The listing agent is not typically the one that referred the borrower, but they have a lot at stake in the transaction. If you appear to be doing something special, like keeping the listing agent informed, they recognize that your level of service is higher than they are used to experiencing. They are also invested in your work so this a perfect time to try to establish a relationship with them. If you impress with your work, there's an opportunity for them to send some of their buyers your way in the future. I always add all of the listing agents on our transactions into our agent database.

Become Recognized As an Expert in Your Field

A powerful way to stand out as an expert as a mortgage professional is to become an educator for your market. This can take a number of forms, but I have concentrated on being an instructor for real estate agent classes. All agents need to attend a certain amount of Continuing Education (CE) classes to maintain their licenses. I have been certified as an instructor and teach real estate CE classes for American Real Estate University. Recently I developed and wrote the materials for a new class, Mortgage 101, which was approved by the State of Georgia and is sponsored by the Board of Realtors®. I'm also invited in to teach parts of some classes where I elaborate on changes in the mortgage industry.

As the instructor of these classes, I'm viewed as a professional and very knowledgeable in the field of mortgages. Because teaching positions me as an expert, almost every time I teach a class, I gain at least one new referral source. Teaching also keeps my name and my company's name in front of lots of agents. People see me and they remember me from their class. Most of the time you don't actually get to speak to them individually at the class, but when people see me another time at an event, they remember me as their instructor. It just opens the door to a lot more avenues for getting referrals. A lot of my success has been based upon doing that, getting out there and teaching classes so people recognize me and my name. I've had real estate offices that asked me to come in to their offices to speak to their whole staff. It might not be a CE course, but I can speak to them for an hour and then all those agents and the staff feel like they know me. Seeing how teaching has opened a lot of new business for me, I have been training other loan officers in our company to do some teaching as well.

About DeAnn Ellis

DeAnn Ellis has been a leader in the mortgage industry for more than eighteen years. She built her expertise in home lending by working for various lenders and even has owned her own mortgage company. She is Senior Loan Officer for Element Funding in Covington, Georgia. DeAnn and her team service all of Georgia.

Through the years, DeAnn has been recognized for her expertise and has earned Top Producer honors. She won the Element Funding President's Club award in 2015 and in 2016 she received the Expert Network Distinguished Mortgage Professional Award™. DeAnn was also featured as a top mortgage professional and on the cover of the December 2015 edition of Top Agent Magazine.

DeAnn is a member of the Chamber of Commerce, East Metro Women's Council of Realtors® and the East Metro Board of Realtors®, where she serves on various committees. She also serves on the board for Action Ministries, an agency established to feed hungry children. DeAnn is also an instructor for American Real Estate University.

For more information about DeAnn Ellis, visit

http://EllisMortgageTeam.com

http://ElementFunding.com/DEllis

https://Facebook.com/Element-Funding-DeAnn-Ellis

https://www.LinkedIn.com/in/DeAnn-Ellis-10418249

MORTGAGE STORM

Joel Comp

Introduction

I'm from Austin, Texas and I started my career working in a sales job at Dell Computers, which was headquartered nearby. I did really well selling computers, but there was something about the rigid structure of a big corporation that didn't suit me. After working there a few years I decided it was time to move onto something else in sales, but I didn't know exactly what I wanted to do. I had recently met a lady in Austin that was moving back to her hometown of San Antonio and she told me about the mortgage business. Her mother, some of her other family members, and friends worked in the industry and said that it might be a good fit for me. I decided I needed a change, so I decided to move to San Antonio and try to get a job in the mortgage industry.

I struggled for a while, interviewing at several large banks and going to job fairs. Nobody would hire me as a mortgage originator because I didn't have any financial industry experience. Finally, after about four months I was able to land a position at a small mortgage brokerage shop, answering the phone. It wasn't the job I wanted, but it got me in the door at a mortgage company, and was a place to start. I began answering the phones, setting up loans, and then moved into processing loans for a couple of years. I then transitioned into originating loans full-time. My career has taken off ever since.

I took the long road with no shortcuts along the way and I really learned all aspects of the mortgage business. I'm happy with the path I chose. I don't think I could have found a better position or industry to be in than the mortgage industry. There's no other way I could be where I am today with my career unless I had chosen to be a doctor, a lawyer, or some other highly skilled professional.

I've been in the mortgage industry for 15 years now and I'm the Executive Vice President and Branch Manager for Gold Financial Services in San Antonio. I originate mortgages for Gold Financial Services in the greater San Antonio area.

Common Obstacles for Loan Officers

Product Knowledge

Product knowledge is the first obstacle a new originator will run into in this industry. They may have a general sense of what a pay stub is, what a W-2 is, or a tax return, but they struggle to have a layered thought process of how these different items interact with each other and contribute to different loan requirements. They don't yet understand what the guidelines and the rules are for a loan, whether it be a conventional Fannie Mae loan, a VA, or FHA loan. As a loan originator you have all these acronyms thrown at you. In the mortgage business it's everyday jargon, but to the average person, they have no clue what it means.

Loan originators also need to understand what the loan process looks like from the very beginning to the end, from loan application all the way through closing. They need to know all the different pieces that are happening in a transaction and all the people that it takes to close it. It takes an army of people to put one single loan together.

The challenge of this industry is that you can't just go to school or take some classes to learn all of this. You have to learn on the job, doing each of these steps yourself until you can master it all. There's almost a sense of secrecy in the mortgage industry. Few people really know what goes on with an actual loan, how it gets securitized, and then put into the secondary market to be bundled and sold. There are a lot of pieces that all need to be done correctly and in the proper sequence from the time a borrower qualifies and signs a loan application, to actually getting the loan closed and the client gets the keys to their house. Originators need to know the whole story so they're able to properly set expectations and provide appropriate advice for their clients.

It takes about two years before a loan originator begins to set the pieces in place and can identify all the pieces to the puzzle. As an originator it's important to understand how to move the pieces around in a way that you can get systems organized in order to get loans closed in an orderly fashion. We rely on other people in related industries and we have to learn how their roles fit into our process. For example, title companies, appraisal offices, attorney's offices, and insurance companies are all a part of our transaction. After a loan originator learns the process, they may have to also educate their business partners on what they are looking for and be able to speak the same language in order to get the answers needed.

As a loan originator the people you're serving, the borrowers as well as the agents on both sides of the transaction and even the sellers, have a lot at stake with the manner in which you conduct your business. The only way that you can be a trusted advisor in this industry is if your partners and clients don't have to worry about their deals, because you, their loan officer and your team, are there taking care of everything, making sure it's all done correctly. With trust, comes repeat business and referrals, turning one loan into maybe three or four loans in the future. It takes a long time, maybe even more than two years, before you can really feel comfortable telling people what the answers are and providing appropriate advice.

Complacency

After becoming a successful loan officer, a common obstacle is complacency and becoming too comfortable with the level of income achieved and the overall feeling that you're doing well enough. The income potential in our industry is almost unlimited, yet most originators never reach anywhere near their potential. They don't see a need to work a little bit harder or smarter and they don't see a need to originate any more loans.

Sometimes this complacency is related to a fear of failure. If a loan officer really puts their full effort into it and nothing changed, I think they would feel it as more of an embarrassment and more of a disappointment for them. Others may also not put in the extra effort that they know they need to do, because they're afraid of what might happen. Loan officers may get into the mentality of, "I did pretty good without really trying," or "You know, I've been doing this three or four years and I'm making a pretty good income, and heck, I didn't even really put my full effort into it. It's pretty good, right?" I believe this attitude of complacency is what holds most originators back.

Value of Mentoring and Coaching

As I mentioned earlier, loan officers pretty much have to learn all of the things they need through on the job experience. Like sharpened steel, if you can be around other successful people, it's much more likely that you're going to be successful as well. It's frequently said, "You are the company that you keep." If you're around and asking questions to people that are more successful than you, you're going to be learning a lot. You can even learn from just listening to successful loan officers' conversations. If you are associated with someone that is modeling what you're aspiring to be, then you should try to immerse yourself in that environment. This gets into the topic of finding a mentor, especially early in your career, to help you learn how to be an excellent loan officer.

Early in my career I worked for a small mortgage shop in San Antonio, which has since grown onto the multi-state mortgage banking firm where I'm currently Executive Vice President. Initially I was answering the phones and then setting up loan packages. My objective was to work my way up to a mortgage originator, but I needed to learn the business basics. I asked to specifically sit outside of my boss's office so I could learn from hearing his conversations. As we got bigger, we moved to different offices, where I would make sure that I was literally right outside his office, so I could hear his phone conversations. That's really where I developed some of my skills. I could hear the back-and-forth conversations that he had with clients; it was somewhat like role-playing, listening to all of the conversations. I was able to hear how a seasoned professional takes every situation and empathizes with it and understands it, and then tells the client how it's going to be handled. I was able to hear the tone and the cadence in his voice. That allowed me to replicate it, and so my mentorship began there.

To hear somebody who's been down that road many, many times was very beneficial to me as I learned certain phrases that were used with borrowers to soothe a variety of situations. I would highly recommend for someone new to the business to find a company to work for that's going to be able to set expectations, honor them, have access to education, and have access to expert leadership. Look for a company that's got people with longevity, those that have been there for ten or fifteen years and haven't left.

I was given the title of Executive Vice President and with that title came the role of working with other branch managers around Texas at our company and sharing with them some of the insights on what we do. I also am available to them to reach out to when they have a problem or a concern on their files. Within my branch office, we have about twenty loan officers and I conduct coaching sessions throughout the month in small groups. Each of the loan officers participates in two coaching sessions per month where we discuss how to grow their own business and how to keep up on all of the technical aspects of the mortgage industry.

Keys to Success As a Mortgage Originator

Build a Great Reputation and Systematically "Wow" Your Clients With Great Service

In order to get more clients, the best strategy is to "wow" them one-by-one, impressing them and your referral partners with a superior level of service. The business should be based on service and technical efficiency. That's something very few originators strive to do. Reliability, honesty, and integrity are all important factors as well. If you treat everyone fairly and the same way that you would your own family, I believe success is guaranteed. In my business we really try to make every client or referral source feel important. When the phone rings, it is answered. Emails are also promptly responded to.

The main aspect is to be available. If you are the one that is available, you'll be there to answer referral partner or client questions and they won't have to call the next person on their list. This is one of the best ways to gain an advantage over the competition and get additional business. People are amazed and wowed if they call early in the morning or in the evening to reach you and they can get their questions answered.

Another important aspect is to keep your clients updated on the status of their loans. My observations are that for the most part loan officers don't keep their clients up to date on the loan status. It's a stressful time for the borrowers and the agents involved in the transaction, so it's better not to let them guess what is happening with the loan. My policy has been to provide a weekly update to everyone involved so they can know where the loan stands every week and what to expect.

Lastly, closing dates are not a movable target; they are actual contractual obligations that need to be honored. I think that's a big miss at a lot of mortgage companies. They may think, "Oh, we'll just move the closing date back two days." That's not something that can be done easily. Buyers and sellers have movers scheduled, are taking off work, and need to have utilities transferred. There can also be money tied up that the seller is going to use for another transaction. And then there is the commission for the agents. Loan officers need to do everything possible to make sure closing happens on time.

My team and I work very hard to be known to honor expectations, and do what we say and say what we mean. If we say, "I'm going to send you your disclosures out today," then we're going to send them out that day. If we say, "We're going to have your file approved by this day," then that's what we do.

Knowledge of Underwriting Standards

A real important key to effectively originating is to understand the guidelines and underwriting standards. Loan officers need to be able to know quickly if a client will qualify for a mortgage. A lot of this depends on the lender you are working for. In my company, we are a mortgage banker. We've got over a dozen underwriters here, but we're still a small enough company that allows us to make our own decisions. We can put our heads together and speak directly with FHA, VA, USDA, Fannie, or Freddie and find out if the agency will allow the loan. I have picked up most of my real estate agent partners over the years because I was able to fix a deal that couldn't be done somewhere else. It wasn't necessarily because the loan was bad, but because it took a little bit more creativity to put it together. I think that comes with knowledge and experience, but it also comes from working for a company that has the ability to do that. We've been able to do things that other lenders can't get done because they're either too stringent with their own underwriting overlays or are just not knowledgeable enough to get it done.

To be able to tell somebody, "yes," and really mean it is really powerful. Often, you've got to really dive into the file and know exactly what you're talking about to make sure you can say, "Yes." I think loan officers say, "No," too often and sometimes our borrowers are painted with the same broad brush. Much of the time the answer should probably be, "Maybe, let me check it out and see." Then you do the research and see if the borrow will qualify.

Experience is often the best teacher. It gives you the test first and the lesson later. You learn a lot of lessons from your mistakes, and you're going to make some of them in this business. Don't be afraid to make a mistake. The thing is to be able to recover from it honestly and rapidly. Fix the problem right away, address it, and move on.

Develop a Base of Referral Partners

As a loan officer, generally the most important source of clients is referral by real estate agents. My first action as a mortgage originator was to meet with and try to establish a base of real estate agent referral sources. There are many different ways of approaching agents, such as meeting them at networking, social events, and inviting them to lunch and drinks. This may prove successful for some people; however, I'm not personally big on social events to meet agents. I want to do business with agents that are working full time in a career and are successful and that don't need me to take them out for lunch, or need me to take them to go have drinks in order to work together. I look for people to work with that want to refer business to me because I'm getting their clients' loans closed and because their clients have a great experience working with me. These agents have their own personal lives outside of business and they don't necessarily need me to be a part of it.

An often-ignored way to build up a base of agent referral partners is maintaining a good communication with the listing agent on a transaction. Referrals typically originate from the agent assisting the buyers, but the listing agent has a lot at stake as well. I always establish communications with the listing agent early in the process and provide the same weekly update to them as the borrower and the borrower's agent. As soon as the client is referred, I call the listing agent and let them know how I work and how I communicate. As the listing agent sees that you do a great job, better than most loan officers, you are likely to garner another referral partner that will refer borrowers when they are on the buying side of transactions.

The other thing to do is to make the referral process work in both directions. I don't just go to real estate agents to find out what they can do for me and get their mortgage leads. I want to have more of a mutual cooperation arrangement, where we can both benefit from referrals. We have established preferred lender programs with local businesses where we get leads of people looking for a house who will need both an agent and a mortgage. We refer these potential clients to our network of agent partners.

About Joel Comp

Joel Comp is the Executive Vice President of Gold Financial Services, a Texas-based mortgage lender. He is also Branch Manager for the San Antonio Branch. Joel has been involved in the mortgage industry for the past fifteen years.

For more information about Joel Comp, visit

http://www.TheCompFactor.com

Brad Cohen

Introduction

I started out in my own business when I was only thirteen years old. I was motivated to make money and save up to buy a car when I reached sixteen. I started a car wash business, initially just washing cars in my neighborhood. By the time I was sixteen, I had saved enough to buy a 1984 Toyota Celica GTS, and I continued to save enough for half of my college education. I continued the business, expanding into detailing and branching out over a little wider area around Potomac and Bethesda, Maryland. After college I did this full time, and I developed a great customer base that included corporate executives, landscapers, paving contractors, investment bankers, and other wealthy clients. I learned a lot through my car wash and detailing business. Many lessons still apply to how I do business today, allowing me to be super successful.

By the age of twenty-five I was doing very well, but I realized this was a tough business—long hours of physical work, and the local weather being what it was, made it a seasonal business. I decided to sell the business and valuable customer list and find something else to do. My stepfather was in the computer industry as a manager of 1,000 sales people. He always told me that the best job to have is a job in sales because there's an unlimited earning potential. He had people working for him in their 30s that were making seven figures per year, so I decided I wanted to find a job in sales.

As I was selling the car wash and detailing business, a good friend of mine introduced me to three people he knew that had recently started a mortgage company in the area. I interviewed with them, and they indicated that they wanted to hire me. At first, I wasn't really excited about the mortgage industry because it was dealing with an intangible product. In contrast, when I was cleaning cars, I'd immediately see the fruits of my labor. I didn't do anything about the offer, but sometimes fate takes over and gives you another chance. I had just sold my business, and I was training the people that had purchased it. We stopped at a bagel shop to pick something up for breakfast and I ran into the three owners of the mortgage company right there at the bagel shop. They told me again that they thought I would be a great fit to work at their mortgage company. I went to meet with them again one more time, and I decided to give this business a try. Obviously, I didn't know anything about the mortgage industry, but I went in and I learned.

I've now been in the mortgage business for twenty years and it's been a great ride. I'm a Senior Mortgage Banker with Capital Bank in Bethesda, Maryland and I originate loans in every state in the country.

Keys to Success As a Loan Officer

Learn the Business

If you're just starting out in the mortgage business, you have to learn how it works and the best way to do that is by working side-by-side with an experienced originator. In my case, I would sit with my manager every morning, and I just listened to everything she said on the phone. She was on a speakerphone, and she'd be fielding phone calls from people that were making inquiries about mortgages, mostly relating to re-financing. I was able to hear both sides of the conversation and the manner in which she asked questions of the applicants. This way I was able to hear all the different scenarios and listen to how she would structure the loans. After a while, I would give her my thoughts on how I thought the loans should be structured, and she would provide feedback. This was a great way to learn quickly because my manager had a lot of business, and I was able to experience how to handle a whole variety of situations in a short period of time. My afternoons were spent on marketing to try to find my own customers.

Although there's not much in the way of formal school training for mortgage loan officers, there are a number of seminars available that cover marketing and systems to help achieve effectiveness. I recommend that new loan officers invest in themselves to learn as much as they can to be successful in this industry.

Develop Great Interpersonal Skills

As in most sales jobs, loan officers need to have excellent interpersonal skills. You're going to be dealing with people from all walks of life, and it's all about how you interact with people, treating every single person with respect. My foundation for this was the years in my car detailing business. I had a great range of clients, and many were corporate CEO's and other very high net worth individuals. I was much younger than my clients, and I really learned the value of being able to relate to all types of people, starting at a young age. One also needs to be very responsive, following up on phone calls and emails. If you're not responding fast enough, clients will be contacting the next loan officer on their list.

Become a Trusted Advisor

Buying a house is usually the largest investment a family will make, and the choice made on the mortgage financing has a long-term impact on a family's overall financial situation. There are a wide variety of terms, such as 15, 20, or 30 years, as well as fixed and variable rates. As a loan officer, you need to be able to properly analyze a borrower's situation, future plans, and goals in order to recommend the best mortgage for your borrower. A key point is being honest with your clients.

Going back to my days of washing and detailing cars, some people would ask if their car needed a full detail or if they could get away with a wash and wax. Although they could afford a full detail, if I believed they really didn't need the detail yet, I would let them know. In mortgages, it's providing the best advice for each client based on their individual circumstances and everyone is different. It's going back to telling the truth and treating the customer's money as if it's your own. My motto is, "If you watch the pennies, your dollars take care of themselves." Just do for people as you would do for yourself. Don't put somebody into a loan that you wouldn't put your own mother into.

Our job as an originator and advisor to our clients is to let them know what mortgage makes the most sense. Sometimes when considering refinancing, staying with what they have may be the best decision for the client, even if you don't make anything. If someone has a 15-year loan and they're three years into it and they are considering refinancing again to another 15-year, you need to do the math and figure out whether or not it makes sense for them to do it again. There's no point in starting somebody over again if they're going to end up spending thousands more in interest payments, just because they're going to save maybe $250 a month right now.

I consider some of my own life lessons when advising clients. When I was thirty-five, I had my father's custom building firm build our dream house. We wanted to make changes and add more to the extent that the house went $441,000 over budget. This made me panic, trying to figure out how to make the payments. Fortunately, interest rates dropped, and I became intensely focused on paying down the mortgage as fast as possible. It was quite a humbling experience to consider that I was giving advice to my customers, and yet I have this big payment on a house I refused to cut back on during the construction. This made me motivated even more to pay it off and on my 40th birthday, I gave a present to myself, writing the last check to pay off the mortgage. This is a great life lesson that I have told hundreds of times so my clients will not make the same mistake I did. Most borrowers think they want a 30-year amortized loan because the common advice is to stretch out the payments as long as possible to get the tax benefits, but I generally recommend a shorter term. In the end it's generally better to have no mortgage payment earlier than the tax benefits that don't really make that much difference.

Around 2004 to 2006, a lot of people in this industry got so greedy and they put people in loans that they should never have been in. There were all of these 100% financing, stated income, stated asset, bad credit loans that many mortgage companies offered. Some had a pick a pay amount loan, pay option ARMs that were good for certain people, but for most people, they were just a disaster, like a ticking time bomb. With the financial meltdown, many of these loans imploded, and all of these bad practices ended and a lot of people got out of the industry. I always stuck with my principles, not putting my clients into the wrong loans that didn't make any sense, and I had some of my best years during and immediately after the financial crises because there was significantly less competition.

One also needs to maintain communications with the clients, whether it's good news or bad news and be upfront on the expectations. If you need the business returns, or you need the tax returns, tell them. Don't sugarcoat the processing requirements and then tell them at the last minute that you need something else. I always send my clients a checklist of what I need immediately. I tell them, "This process may be painful but it's going to be less painful if you get me this documentation up front versus piecemeal. It's a financial colonoscopy. We're going to cross the finish line together. Let's work together and get this documentation, and we'll get this loan approved as fast as possible."

Marketing

Marketing is critical for any business and there are so many ways to approach marketing for clients in the mortgage industry. One critical point is that you have to be a self-starter. Conventional wisdom says to try to establish referral relationships with real estate agents and to start out contacting everyone you know or have done business with in the past to start attracting clients; but this didn't seem to be a good fit when I was starting out.

My mother is a real estate agent, and she actually discouraged me from getting into the mortgage business. She didn't think I would be very good at it. Not only that, she said she wouldn't even refer me a single deal until I knew what I'm doing. She didn't want me messing up any of her transactions or ruining her relationships. She did say that, if after one year I could prove to her that I knew what I was doing, then she would share her database. Her reaction gave me a drive to prove her wrong, and it also persuaded me to find another way to find clients.

Also, I didn't believe I could initially go after my car wash clientele, because these people were mostly wealthy people of Potomac, Bethesda, and Washington, D.C. I didn't think all of a sudden they were going to let some kid that was washing and detailing their car for the past few years figure out what's the best mortgage for them and to handle all of their personal information. I knew that wasn't going to happen, and that I had to first prove to these people that I knew what I was doing.

I knew I had to find a way to make the phone ring and even though I had a college degree from Ithaca, I was only twenty-five years old and not too many people want someone that young and inexperienced handling their financial affairs. I wondered how I was going to get people to find me. I also had a hard time just

actually saved some people from foreclosure. I also tell them that I've saved some people from having to sell their house for a loss and thus preserved the value of all the homes in the neighborhood.

Build a Referral-based Business

One of the most important success formulas is to build up a business that is based on repeat business and referrals from past clients and other sources. A lot of loan officers don't think about the long-term success of their business and just chase new customers. I look at my customers in a different way—potentially each one of my customers can send me ten referrals over a lifetime and their value is so much higher than just the transaction at the moment. Growing a business with referrals just makes it easier every year. Today about 80% of all my business comes from referrals.

The first step is to capture all of your customer information and load it into a database. I started doing this as I was closing loans from my first year. After every single transaction, I would hand write a thank you letter to every single borrower and stick two business cards in that envelope. I then put key information into my database and have continued to add to it year-after-year. To be effective, you need to stay in touch with the people in your database. This can be accomplished by frequently sending useful information and thanks for referrals. There are a variety of tools to automate the process, including database software tailored to the mortgage industry and auto-responders to automate the email process. It's amazing the power of these tools, where with a few clicks, you can send out an email to thousands of your fans.

Establishing relationships with business professionals can be a good source of referrals. Most originators focus their efforts on establishing referral partnerships with real estate agents, but there are also many other people that can be referral sources, like insurance agents, financial planners, and attorneys.

I've always had real estate agents send me business because they knew I did a great job, but I've never specifically gone after them for their business. Agents expect that if they send you business, that you're going to send them business, but it's already past that stage by the time I get my clients. My clients have already found a house or know who they're working with to find them the house. They just want to find the money by the time they come to me. The other thing is that in this stage of my career, I don't want to work nights and weekends anymore, when agents want you to be available. Saturday morning is the time that I like to get up early and spend about three or four hours outside washing my cars. I'm a clean fanatic when it comes to my cars, and that's my time to just decompress.

I can be a great referral source for other businesses, so that's where I have focused my efforts. I have an insurance agent that I refer five to ten leads a week. I refer a moving company leads all the time. One attorney at a large law firm has sent me over seventy customers in the past four years, almost all of them attorneys in his firm.

About Brad Cohen

Brad Cohen is a Senior Mortgage Banker with Capital Bank in Bethesda, Maryland. With twenty years in the mortgage industry, he participated in the development of the mortgage division at Capital Bank. Brad is a top-producing originator, specializing in mortgage lending with competitive rates and exceptional customer service.

Brad has personally closed in excess of 3 billion dollars in residential mortgages in his career, and 80% of his business comes from past clients and referrals. He is the top originator at Capital Bank and in 2011 was ranked as No. 5 nationally by Scotsman Guide's Top Originators. He was ranked No.8 nationally in 2012, No. 25 nationally in 2013 and No. 11 nationally by Scotsman Guide's Top Originators.

Brad got his start in business at an early age, starting his own car wash and detailing business at only thirteen. He saved up enough money by the time he was sixteen to purchase a car and he was able to expand the business. He earned enough cleaning cars to pay for half of his college education. Brad learned a lot of lessons in business and interpersonal relationships while owning his business that he still applies today as a top-producing mortgage professional.

For more information about Brad Cohen, visit

http://www.0Points.com

https://www.Facebook.com/Bradley.S.Cohen.7

MORTGAGE STORM

Jason Gosser

Introduction

Both of my parents were real estate agents and my father became a real estate appraiser, so a lot of our family conversations as I was growing up were about real estate. My first job was in construction, but from an early age I had dollar signs in my eyes and knew I would never be satisfied in any type of labor position, so I considered getting involved in sales. If it wasn't mortgages, it probably would've been real estate, or some other sales-type position.

I had an interview with a mortgage office manager that knew my mother. Of course, being 100% commission, it's not too terribly difficult to get a job. He hired me, put me on a fast-track, and told me exactly what I had to do to be successful. I spent a lot of my time visiting real estate offices the old-school way, knocking on doors and introducing myself. I was financially motivated and really wanted to make a mark and do well in the industry, and in life. Being only twenty-two at the time, it took quite a while for people to take me seriously, but I just kept at it and things started to evolve.

In 1994, there was a blip in the market and rates went up. That was when I realized that I needed be more established and to save some money. Making as much money as possible became my primary focus for the next several years and I continued to grow both my business and my bank account. Of course, I'm older now, and wiser, and I get my inspiration in other areas, not just money. Now my primary driver is that I love to see other people succeed, and I work hard to provide opportunities for others to succeed and thrive in my organization.

I've been involved in the mortgage industry for over twenty years now. Today, I'm the Branch Manager for Guild Mortgage Company in Everett, WA. The majority of my loans originate in the greater Seattle area, but I'm also licensed and originate loans in a number of other states as well. In addition to my duties as a mortgage originator and branch manager, I also have a private mortgage coaching practice where I coach both loan officers and inside sales agents (dialers) with my team building coach and business partner Isaac Stegman.

Common Obstacles For Loan Officers

Difficulty Finding a Mentor and Getting Training

One of the obstacles as you get involved in the mortgage industry is to really dig in and learn the business. There's really not much in the way of formal training available, so it's up to you to find a way to learn what you have to know. The best way to start is to find someone that can mentor and coach you, giving you the benefit of their years of experience and often providing you with some sort of accountability.

Over the past ten years, a lot of loan officers who were able to weather the financial storm have, in my opinion, become too focused on themselves and simply staying in survival mode. They haven't really been thinking about expanding, growing, leveraging, mentoring, or training. It seems to be about making as much money as they can, just paying their bills and nothing more. A lot of loan officers are also operating from a scarcity mindset and don't want to share information or mastermind with others in the industry. Most try to hoard all the relationships and information, which is contrary to how I operate.

If you're just getting started, I would suggest trying to find somebody to work for that has a proven track record of success and is willing to mentor and coach you. Interview with different companies and talk with different people, because you want to be working with someone who is willing to take the time to teach you step-by-step exactly how to be successful and who has achieved or surpassed the level of success you want to attain.

Starting Out, You Need to Have Cash to Sustain the Early Months With Little to No Income Until You Get Established

Most people don't have enough money to jump right into a commission-only job. In this industry, you start from scratch, building relationships and closing loans. It can be really difficult to establish relationships with real estate agents because they already have relationships with other mortgage originators. It takes a long time to meet someone, get to know them, call on them again and again, go to lunch, have coffee, and then maybe finally get a referral out of it. By the time that referral manifests into a transaction, and closes, and then you get paid, it could be four, five, six months later, if everything lines up perfectly.

Industry Standards Are Generally Not Set Very High

Most loan officers are not top producers. They may provide good service, but for some reason they can never seem to break through to the place where they are doing big numbers. Most of the time this has to do with the environment that they are in and the standards and expectations that are set. It's often said, "You are only as good as the people you hang out with." That certainly applies in the mortgage business or in any sales job for that matter. If you are surrounding yourself with people who do a certain volume of business, a lot of times you get stuck at that level. That's what seems "normal" to you. What you want to do is to surround yourself with people who have set very high standards and expectations for themselves and you will bring yourself up to their level.

Value of Mentors and Coaches

One of my first managers, Ken Allen, was also my first mentor. He's somebody that gave me a lot of guidance and help. He had a great business and I looked up to him, so I wanted to emulate him. I wanted to do the kind of business that he did. He was such a kind, awesome person and he was also able to keep me motivated and teach me how to succeed in this business. Today, he's one of my competitors, but we are also lifelong friends.

After I spent some time in the business and learned everything I could from him, I pretty much trail-blazed my own way until I found coaching. I have a personal coach who has been working with me for a number of years now. He's an incredible mentor, so much so that I consider him more of a life coach. I run a lot of things by him and he's been instrumental in changing my life and keeping me grounded and stable. In the last four or five years, I've become a firm believer in coaching for various aspects of life and business. I have a fitness coach now as well as a life coach, and in 2015 I added Jeff Latham and Isaac Stegman as business and team building coaches. Since then my business has grown from approximately 100 million in 2014 to 163 million in 2015 to being on pace for over 200 million in 2016, and Isaac and I have now partnered to start coaching other loan originators who want to model what I've done to grow my team! I can honestly say that I firmly believe in the power of coaching and consider it one of the best investments I can make in my life and business.

I spend a lot of my time now masterminding with other successful loan originators and business owners, sharing our thoughts and ideas and supporting one another. We also provide accountability for each other in meeting the goals we set for our businesses. We piggyback off one another to propel ourselves into more success and live better lives, making sure that we're doing the things that we need to do to achieve our goals.

Often, people are their own worst enemies, because they don't know what to do or exactly how to do it to be successful. Sometimes it's a lack of structure, or maybe they're not organized enough, or they simply lack the discipline or some necessary skill required to take it to the next level. I think again that's where coaching comes into play. Coaching is so important, especially in the real estate and mortgage industry, because it helps you to get through where you're stuck. It helps you in areas that need improvement and just as importantly, provides accountability. It helps set a new standard because your coaches are more advanced in some area and are generally doing more business than you are doing or have figured out how to do something you haven't been able to do on your own.

I have a recipe for success where I can take just about anybody who wants to be successful, and I can make them successful. The key point is if they really want to be successful, they have to stick to the plan and be willing to work hard. Most people don't have that discipline. They get sidetracked and allow the rest of their life derail them. They lose focus and get caught up in things that distract them from making progress. It's just like losing weight. People have to want to lose weight. You can go to a gym all you want, be surrounded by healthy people, and it doesn't mean you're going to lose weight. A lot of it you have to do on your own. You have to go home, you have to eat right and work out. You can't just rely on other people to do it for you.

This business is really not that complicated, from a sales standpoint. I think we often hold ourselves back, and to move forward I suggest you do what I have done and work with a coach that is going to help you lay out a road map to success and that will help push you through your own barriers. Those people who throw themselves into their work, hold high expectations, have a system for accountability, and are really motivated, are the people that are going to succeed. It's actually pretty simple. When the phone rings, pick it up. When you need prospects, pick up the phone. Pick up the phone, constantly, over, and over, and over again. Go out and build relationships. Take care of your clients. Ask for business, then take good care of them and earn the right to ask for referrals. Get up every day and do the right thing versus the easy thing. That's where you will see a tremendous amount of success.

Keys to Success As a Mortgage Originator

The "Why" and Purpose

The first step for anybody who wants to join this industry is, they need to define their "why" and their purpose. When you're in sales you have to know why you are doing what you're doing.

Personally, I get incredible satisfaction from defining my "why." I get to be a part of changing not only the lives of the people that work for me, but we also team up with numerous charities where we are able to contribute and help local children that are displaced from their homes and also help children in other countries who have very little chance at a good life. You can visit the following sites to find out more about these organizations:

www.SellAHomeSaveAChild.org, or

www.CocoonHouse.org

Purposeful Conversations with Referral Partners Need to Be a Non-negotiable Part of Every Week

Picking up the phone and having purposeful conversations with referral partners, over and over again, is one of the keys to my business success. I think that comes from time-blocking these periods weekly as non-negotiable time, where no matter what you do your prospecting and other business-building tasks, and you do not deviate from that. You need to make a certain number of prospecting calls each and every week based on your production goals. If that's your foundation and you develop great habits that support your success, amazing things are going to happen from just that one item alone.

A "non-negotiable" is a very powerful term when you use it for the purpose of setting yourself up with goals. Let's say a goal might be to make fifty contacts in a week with referral partners. Your non-negotiable is twenty. You don't leave on Friday until you've hit that non-negotiable. Now, if you find that you don't hit your non-negotiable over a couple of weeks, then you need to review the target and possibly scale back, but be honest with yourself in understanding what is holding you back. In this business, if you're not doing your basic prospecting, it doesn't really matter what kind of CRM you have, it doesn't matter how cool the app on your phone is. Nothing else is relevant if you're not making your contacts because pretty soon your pipeline will be empty and you won't be seeing a paycheck for a while.

Work With Partners That Are a Good Fit for How You Want to Do Business

As you're out there prospecting, you'll find real estate agents, maybe even top-producing agents, and immediately know they are not going to be a good fit. It may be because they expect you to be at all of their Saturday and Sunday open houses when you have family obligations, or that they want you to spend all of your time calling their cold leads for them. I've met many agents that haven't been a good fit, and I've respectfully turned down the opportunity to work with them because they didn't fit within my model. But that hasn't held me back at all. All I did was pick up the phone and find other agents that I did see eye-to-eye with, people that would enhance my life. One of the things that I try to tell my team is if you're constantly prospecting, you have lots of opportunities to say "yes" or "no." Otherwise, you might be in the situation where you'll say, "yes," just because you feel you need the money, even when the things they want you to do conflict with how you want to live your life.

Choose to be in the position where you are in control of your business, and you get to say "yes" only when you want to say "yes." You don't want to be desperate. When you engage in a relationship that's not healthy for your business, it takes away from your ability to attract healthy relationships that are good for your business. You lose time and it takes a toll on your attitude. It's counterproductive and you will eventually end up losing money on the relationship.

Develop a Good System to Track Your Clients and Stay in Touch

There's a rule of thumb that you need three times the amount of money to market to a new client, than you do marketing to your past client. If you put some effort and energy into your past clients, you can get three times the return. That's something that we've really focused on. Since the day I started, I've maintained a constant database where I kept the names and numbers of every one of my past clients. There were times in my career when the market really tightened up and I was able to bounce back from that more aggressively than I normally would, and pull out referrals and business from past clients, especially for refinancing.

Maintaining past clients has been really, really important to me. Anytime one of our clients refers someone to us, we consider the referring client to be a VIP client and we send them a gift card and a thank you note. We try to do such a good job for them that they choose to refer us because they want their friend or colleague to get the best service possible.

Breaking Through the "Tipping Point"

When you continue to succeed and grow, you eventually get to the point where you don't have the personal capacity to do any more. A lot of successful loan officers are in constant chaos and they are working lots of hours. They're making good money, but they're afraid to leverage themselves and hire new people to help. Many have a fear about going out and hiring people, because they are afraid of the financial commitment and often they don't think they can find anyone who will do as good a job with their clients as they would.

When I was doing high volume by myself, I was making great money, but I was working sixty, seventy hours a week and missing out on a lot of the things that are important to me, like spending time with my family. A big key to my success comes down to my ability to leverage. I learned how to leverage myself through partnering with loan officers on my team where we build mutually beneficial relationships with referral partners.

I refer to this as the "tipping point." After being stuck at a certain level, I broke through that ceiling and now I can produce a lot more without sacrificing the other things that are important to me.

One of the big things we teach our coaching clients is how to effectively build a team and push through that tipping point. I'm doing more business now than I ever have in my life. I was number twenty-seven last year in mortgage volume in the country and am now working less than forty hours a week! I was able to punch through the tipping point and I have that ability to hire enough staff because of the production volume that I do. I've learned how paying super talented people to work for me helps me grow the business, even if it's dipping into my pocket. I leverage myself with partners; I call them partnering loan officers. Because I'm only one person, I can only have so many relationships with agents and I can only call so many people, but once I figured out the formula for successfully partnering, the sky is the limit.

As soon as I started to leverage myself, I realized I was working less hours and doing twice the volume than I'd ever done. That is where a lot of people get stuck, at that tipping point. In my coaching I encourage people to take the risk and find talented people to help them grow their own dream, then I show them step-by-step exactly how to do that!

If You Are Established and Have the Resources, Partner With Real Estate Agents to Use Telemarketing to Find Mortgage Business and Real Estate Clients for the Agents

One resource I can't live without is my dialers or what we call inside sales agents on my team. A lot of times we will team up with real estate agents to try to find mortgage business for us, as well as real estate clients for the agents. It's been a really effective tool in growing our business.

Most real estate agents don't have the support staff to constantly be dialing. They're out selling houses, they're in the car, and they're showing. They could lose a day or two, or three days, or a week, just working with one client, and meanwhile they're not prospecting and those leads are getting cold. By partnering our telemarketing efforts with agents, we're prospecting right alongside them.

I have top-producers from all over the country flying out to Washington to meet me, because I'm the number one guy in my company. They heard about our dialer program and wanted to find out what I was doing that made it a success. I hosted days with four or five of the top people, who are also friends of mine before finally coming to the conclusion that this format was really counterproductive to what I'm trying to do. It takes away my time and theirs and they just went back with little pieces of what I do versus the whole picture. They didn't really get the foundation, because they were here for only a few hours, and trying to absorb it all and then effectively implement it in their own business simply takes a lot more time.

What I decided to do at that point was partner with Isaac and my lead ISA on another coaching program specifically for loan originators who wanted to duplicate my model and use inside sale agents. I have my lead inside sales agent doing coaching calls once a week with other inside sales agents. She works on scripting and accountability and assigns them projects. In this way other loan officers don't have to learn the system themselves and their dialers can get the very best training and accountability available.

If you can get a properly trained inside sales agent who's prospecting for you forty hours a week, fifty-two weeks a year, their salary plus the coaching cost is a drop in the bucket. If they're making sixty to eighty calls a day, that's anywhere from three to four hundred calls a week, times fifty-two. That's thousands of calls that you weren't able to make. As an originator, we can make anywhere from three to five thousand dollars on any one particular transaction. That person would then be responsible to make you one more deal per month to cover their salary and coaching cost, which is a no-brainer, and the rest is icing on the cake!

About Jason Gosser

Jason Gosser is the Branch Manager for Guild Mortgage Company in Everett, Washington. Jason has over twenty years of experience in the mortgage industry and he is licensed to originate mortgages in Arizona, California, Colorado, Georgia, North Dakota, Oregon, South Carolina, Tennessee, and Washington.

Gosser is the #1 Loan Originator for Guild Mortgage Company and is also #1 in Washington State, with a projected $230 million in sales volume for 2016. According to The Scotsman Guide 2015, Team Gosser is #1 in the country for FHA loans.

Jason is married to his beautiful wife Chilly and they have two amazing kids. The Gossers live in Lake Stevens, Washington but spend most of their summers in Crescent Bar, Washington on the Columbia River. Jason says that 90% of his motivation to crush it in lending comes from the freedom it provides to spend more time with his family.

For more information on Jason or his team, visit:

www.JasonGosser.com, or

www.Facebook.com/TeamGosser

The Action Group is part of Kaizen Coaching and focuses on teaching Loan Originators how to successfully build high-producing teams with great culture without sacrificing quality of life. For more information, visit:

www.TheActionGroup1.com

MORTGAGE STORM

Justin Oliver

Introduction

After graduating from Arizona State University I followed my passion and ventured into a job at a large financial firm as a financial advisor. It was challenging but also a stimulating experience that had me fall in love with the financial industry.

After about three months from graduation I was about to secure my Series 7 when the unfortunate events of September 11th happened. At that time it made it very hard for a kid out of college to convince wealthy investors to invest their investable assets with me. I got by and did pretty well for a few tough years working a lot of hours. During this same time interest rates were falling to all-time lows and I had a few friends that were in the mortgage industry. After talking to a few of them (one my partner still today) and finding out how well they were doing it got me thinking that I should take my career in a different direction. I had invested in real estate starting back in college, and with a good understanding of the GSE's and mortgage-backed securities, it was a natural progression toward the real estate or mortgage industry. Because my girlfriend at the time (now my wife of 11 years) was a real estate agent I decided to stick with numbers and pursue the mortgage arena!

In 2003 the tremendously low rates made it an easy start in a new industry. Many people were refinancing at the time and it seemed like my phone was constantly ringing off the hook with new business. Then came 2004 to 2006 with one of the hottest housing markets in the country right here in Phoenix. That's when I decided there was a great opportunity to build a long-term residual business. So I started working more on the home purchase side and building relationships, some that I still have today.

I've now been in the mortgage industry for 13 years. I currently am part of the Oliver-Whalen Team with my partner Ryan Whalen and run a 100 million+ a year team. We also run a large branch in Gilbert, Arizona for NOVA Home Loans.

Common Obstacles for Loan Officers

Learning the Standards for Lending and Being Compliant

Back in 2003 when I got started it seemed like pretty much anyone could get a loan. Regulations and requirements for qualifying for a loan have become much tighter in recent years and frequently change. Loan officers today need to stay on top of all the changes and also need to understand how to structure a loan that best meets the needs of their clients. This includes having a good understanding of the parameters the Government Sponsored Enterprises (GSEs), like Fannie Mae and Freddie Mac, and the investors will allow. Additionally mortgage originators now have to be licensed, so there is some basic knowledge that needs to be acquired so you can pass the licensing exam.

Mortgage Origination Is Generally 100% Commission-based

The mortgage origination profession has among the highest earning potential of all professions, but it takes time to build up a client base when starting out. Most loan officers' earnings are going to be based 100% on commission, which means you have to have cash on hand to sustain your personal expenses until you build up your business. Commissions on mortgages originated are time-lagged, meaning from the day you get a deal, you're probably not going to get paid on that deal for 45 to 60 days or more. The other thing to consider is there are always going to be ebbs and flows of the business volume. There will be months that are going to be really great and there will be months that are not so great, so building up savings to sustain lean times is going to be critical for long-term survival in this industry.

Trying to Do It All Yourself

As loan officers become successful and ramp up their originations, they frequently reach a level where they get stuck and can't grow beyond that point. This may happen when they are originating about 8 to 12 loans a month. The reality is that there is only so much one person can do, so if you have reached that point, it's time to start building a team to grow your business. Sometimes the loan officer is afraid to give up any ownership of their loan files. Identify and hire good people that are better than you, delegate to them, and trust them. You'll ultimately be able to build a really good team around you, which helps you expand your business.

It's hard to delegate the first time, and it may be hard to do it even the second or third time, but once you learn how to leverage your business, you'll be able to get out of the way of your origination partners and processors. It's tough because you've spent a lot of time establishing relationships with real estate agents and referral partners, and then you are handing over deals to a loan officer on your team. Or, you may be having your processor talk directly to the real estate agent, or to that client you just signed-up.

Once you start leveraging your business, you can move up from 8 to 12 deals a month to 40 or 50. You're not going to grow your business until you get out of the way of your business!

Self-improvement and Coaching

When I got my start in mortgages I didn't know about coaching or that coaching for loan officers even existed. I have always tried to learn as much as possible, and my interest in the financial markets led me to read lots of business and money books. That was initially my path toward self-improvement. One of the first business books I ever read was "Think and Grow Rich" by Napoleon Hill. He talks about a secret in the book—the secret is that you become what you think about the most. That is also my mindset. For the last 13 years—when I'm going to sleep, when I'm waking up—I'm thinking about what I want my business to look like next year, or in five years. Or, I'm thinking of what I want the branch to accomplish. This practice helps me focus on my goals and long-term plan of action.

About five or six years ago I went to a seminar held by a national coaching company and learned many new ways to grow my business. Our team implemented several tactics that were adapted from the seminar training and we are still using most of them today. Even though it is a simple concept, we learned the value of following up and hadn't realized how much business we had been missing due to not having a good follow up process. About two years ago I did hire coaching and that has really helped us with developing a business vision, building faith in a team and knowing our numbers. I've also had great mentors in the people that have been running our company. They are all top loan officers themselves and I have had the honor and benefit of learning much from them.

I always think about a quote by Picasso when I'm planning my business. It says, "Good artists copy. Great artists steal." It's that simple. Loan officers should shadow the top loan officers at their company first and foremost. They should also be getting in contact with the top loan officers in their market and request a half-hour or hour, maybe over lunch, asking them what they do and just listening to what they say. Then copy the best ideas and make it your own.

That's what we've done. Over the last five years, we've just copied some of the systems and procedures we've learned from many top loan officers, because if what they were doing was working, then why wouldn't we do exactly the same things? We've tweaked what we have learned and made it our own. There's never really a good reason to try and reinvent the wheel. The most important part of course is implementing the systems and procedures that you learn. Some loan officers receive good advice and have a sincere desire to improve, but they just don't do anything with it. After you get all that information, you've got to implement it or it doesn't matter and you've just wasted your time.

I conduct informal coaching sessions for originators in my branch and on my team. We talk about learning from the mistakes I made over the years and how to avoid doing exactly the same things. I also share what has worked well for me in my career so that they don't have to figure out everything by themselves. This is just another way to strengthen the team that I rely upon.

Keys to Success As a Mortgage Originator

**Following Our Team Slogan Can Help Any Business:
"Always Available, Eager to Educate, Constant
Communication, and Forever and Follow-up"**

Always Available

In our industry, you have to be available. If you don't pick up the phone, or you don't respond to e-mails then you're going to be losing business. If you personally can't take every call or e-mail then you need to have someone else handling communications as your back up. We have a production coordinator and a transaction coordinator at my office. If I'm busy, or if I'm out of town, they're going to be responding extremely fast. Time is of the essence since our clients usually want to buy fast. If you're not going to get back to them, then they're probably going to move on and find another loan officer to originate their loan. Our goal is to respond within a maximum of five to fifteen minutes. For many, this may sound difficult to achieve, but that's the standard for our team.

Eager to Educate

After we talk to the client, we want to make sure they clearly understand the process toward closing their loan. As a loan officer we may not realize that a first-time homebuyer, or even someone that's a move-up buyer, doesn't always understand what will be happening over the time while their loan is being processed and the details of the program or the product. It's really important to educate them so that they know exactly what they're getting and they walk into the process feeling comfortable. If not, it's bound to go wrong.

Constant Communication

We want all of our clients to know exactly what is going on with their file so we do weekly status updates to our clients on every Monday. We also want to make sure the agents are informed, so we provide a weekly update to them as well every Tuesday. The weekly updates also put pressure on us to keep the files moving along, because we want to make sure we're not calling our clients and the agents seven days later with nothing happening in the past week. That's not a fun call.

Forever and Follow up

Our intention is that our customers are with us forever, but we need to make sure that we remain in front of them. When we close a deal, we'll offer to do a house-warming party to get all their friends to come and see their new house. If they are not interested in a party, we send them something nice that would fit their personality and house as a follow up gift.

sitting in the office making calls because I was always an outdoors person with my previous business. I thought back to how I had attracted customers for a number of years, and it was by distributing flyers and wondered why it wouldn't work for mortgages. I ran this by one of the owners and he thought it was a horrible idea. He said nobody does this. Anyway, I figured it was my responsibility to find a way to bring in business, so I decided to start distributing flyers. After sitting with my manager in the mornings, listening to her handling customers, I started distributing flyers in the afternoons.

I started passing out flyers every single day to certain neighborhoods trying to generate leads for refinancing. My goal was to pass out 2,000 flyers a week. Then the phone started to ring. In my first year in the business, I ended up closing 155 loans and 148 of those were refinances. Even though I was only twenty-five years old, I made $131,000 in that first year, much more than I had ever expected, and I was hooked on this business.

Today, even though most of my business is from referrals, I still use the flyers as a marketing strategy. I generally am getting 50 to 60 new clients per year, just by continuing to use the flyers. It may not be a huge portion of my business, but by hitting the same neighborhoods over and over again, it results in brand awareness. I want the flyer distribution done well and don't want them ending up in storm drains or in the woods, so I pay people well to pass them out. I generally find people on Craig's List and I pay them $17.50 an hour. This is a lot of money for that type of job, but I want it handled properly and with that wage you can get really good people.

The only downside I've seen is that there are always a few people that want to complain about something. I've had a few people call me up and say that they don't like to see the flyers and that they would never use someone who has to resort to flyers for advertising. I may not completely change their minds, but I tell them that I helped forty of their neighbors in the last year and loan partners doing 8 to 12, you can get to that 50, 60, or more deals in a month.

It's also really important to get those loan officer partners to meet and get to know the agents that you're working with. Agents don't like being passed off, but once they understand why you have the team in place and they get to know your loan officer partner, the relationship works well. We have agents that now do not even call me directly. They go to one of my loan officer partners. That sounds like something scary, but that means it's working. I can just go get more real estate agents and my loan officer partner doesn't really need leads from me anymore. They can knock out 10 to 12 deals a month because they have started building these relationships with our referral partners.

Being consistent and predictable as a team is critical when working with referral partners so they know exactly what they're getting and are comfortable working with both you as their loan officer and your team. Agents shouldn't become confused if they are talking to someone on your team versus you; they shouldn't get a different answer. Everyone on the team needs to be trained on policies and procedures and working toward the same goals.

Build Your Brand in the Market

As loan officers expand their business it's important to position as a leader in the market and build brand awareness. This isn't just about branding as the mortgage lending company, but it's about branding the loan officer and team. In our business we're now at the point where we're looking for omnipresence. We've done radio and television commercials, billboards, and also a radio show. We do all of this to stay in front of consumers and real estate agents and make sure they remember us. They see us when they drive by the billboards, or they turn on their TV. We don't necessarily get immediate deals from the advertising, but it elevates our presence in the local market and it's building our brand awareness among both consumers and agents.

165

About Justin Oliver

Justin Oliver graduated from the WP Carey Business School at Arizona State University and has been working in the financial world since 2001. His background and experience includes mortgage brokering/banking, financial advising and money management. Justin held Series 7 and Series 66 securities licenses as well as a real estate license, all which have contributed to his understanding of the financial markets and how they function. He has also been personally involved in more than 2000 residential and commercial real estate sales transactions.

Justin is Vice President and Mortgage Advisor at NOVA Home Loans in Gilbert, Arizona. Along with Partner, Ryan Whalen, he heads the Oliver-Whalen Team at NOVA Home Loans and the Gilbert Branch Office.

Justin's extensive hands on experience provides a significant advantage when working with real estate agents and advising homebuyers on mortgage financing options. He is also certified by the State of Arizona to teach continuing education classes on mortgage financing and the financial markets to agents. He holds a Certified Mortgage Planning Specialist Certification and has been featured in Scotsman Guide and was named in the Top 1% of Mortgage Originators in America.

Justin and Team Partner, Ryan Whalen, host a weekly radio show, "Keeping It Real," about all things related to real estate. The show's goal is to educate listeners about the ever-changing real estate market, and help them make informed decisions by providing accurate and relevant information.

NMLS# 164869
NOVA Home Loans
NMLS# 3087

For more information about Justin Oliver, visit

http://oliverwhalenteam.com

https://www.facebook.com/OliverWhalenTeam

https://www/linkedin.com/in/JustinOliverMortgage

Joe McBreen

....

Introduction

After graduating from college in Ireland, I went to work at The Board of Trade in Chicago, arbitrage trading future contracts for clients. I had a very successful career there until about 2001 when everything became more digitalized in the trading world. I really wasn't trained for that so I decided to look at other opportunities. I had a friend that was working for a new bank in Chicago and he recruited me to work with them and be trained as a mortgage loan officer.

I've now been originating mortgages for fifteen years and have been with Guaranteed Rate for the past five years where I am a Vice President of Mortgage Lending in Chicago. In addition to Illinois, I'm licensed in a number of other states and have built a base of business around the United States assisting investors with loans on their rental properties.

Common Obstacles for Loan Officers

Compliance and Knowledge

Prior to 2008, Wall Street was heavily involved in pooling mortgages and the guidelines had become fairly lax. There were loan products available, which required minimum documentation and/or no income verification, so that made the mortgage industry a lot easier than it is today. Today, Frank-Dodd Wall Street Reform and Consumer Protection Act imposes strict regulations on the financial industry.

As a new loan officer to the industry, one really needs to learn loan program guidelines. It's a challenge to learn, not just the basics so you can become licensed, but to keep up with constantly changing guidelines and to make sure you are always compliant. Product availability changes frequently and some lenders establish credit overlay requirements on top of the lender guidelines. If you keep up with the various guidelines, you'll become more confident in what you're selling and when dealing with a client who might have an unusual situation. Knowledge is key and it will help in growing your business.

Being Too Comfortable With What You Are Achieving

People who have been in the industry for a while sometimes get stuck at a certain level of production. After achieving a certain level of success they become comfortable with their results and don't try to grow their business any further. It can be easy to have a good month, hit your normal target half way through, and feel like you can relax until next month.

One of the mistakes I made earlier in my career was that I focused on loan dollar volume instead of unit volume. Once I hit a certain dollar volume, I knew what my earning potential was for that month and then didn't pay much attention to growing my business again until the following month. I realized I was looking at it completely wrong in terms of how I was measuring my business. I changed my focus to concentrate on closing units and shifted my marketing strategy to increase my unit volume. Every loan needs to be treated the same way, whether it's a $1,000,000 mortgage or a $50,000 mortgage. The execution has to be equally consistent so that we get referred more and more by our past clients. With the focus on closing more units every month, the dollar volume follows.

As I switched gears, I brought in a social media director who created a social media campaign that marketed to my past clients. They are your biggest circle of influence outside of your regular referral base. However, once you've established a successful business, you need to keep growing and nurturing your referral sources. These are generally real estate agents, builders, and other professionals, like financial planners.

Value of Mentoring and Coaching

The mortgage business is one where you pretty much learn everything on the job, as there's not much training available. As you start working in this business you can get up to speed if you work under an experienced, top producing loan officer that's willing to train you. My first loan officer position was at a bank and I had the good fortune to work with a manager that taught me how to be successful. Even the regional manager of the bank at the time was very helpful in showing me how to grow and learn the business as well as how to address issues that come up in the underwriting process. They helped me with that initial growth spurt and over the years they have been colleagues and friends that I can call and swap ideas with. Those relationships are still in place today and will always be strong.

Now that I have a lot of experience and have been able to grow my business, I'm able to help new loan officers that are new to the industry. I've also helped them execute their loans with the support of my processing team. After mentoring them, they generally work with me for a couple of years until they are comfortable working and growing their own business within our company.

Keys to Success for a Loan Officer

Mindset for Success

To have success in the mortgage industry, from a mindset perspective, you have to make a commitment to your business and to developing your craft. This isn't a part-time job and putting in the hours is paramount to success. Reputation is crucial, especially when growing your referral base, and without the consistency of hard work it will be difficult to solidify your reputation in the industry. Being available is another important aspect, especially when you are starting out. Let your referral base know that you will be available on a consistent basis, not just Monday to Friday, nine to five. With virtually everyone connected to mobile devices around the clock, we have an instant gratification society thus customers and referral partners expect you to be available twenty-four seven. If you're not available, someone else will be and will win the deal.

Knowledge of the Guidelines

Lending guidelines are frequently in flux and though it may be difficult keeping up, not providing proper insight and advice would be a disservice to your clients. For example, over-committing to a client when certain guidelines have changed can negatively impact their ability to qualify for a loan. Own up to any mistake and address it quickly. A knowledgeable loan originator will know and understand the different criteria and should be able to recommend the appropriate loan product to a consumer. The best way to learn and master the guidelines is with repetition. As you work through more and more similar loans, you will better understand how the guidelines apply to individual borrowers. In the early stages of your career, I would suggest focusing on a limited number of loan products so you can master each one you offer.

Timely Communications

Along with getting loans processed and executed properly, communication with your borrowers and referral partners is essential. It can be a stressful time for the client and the agents on both sides of a purchase transaction need to have the loan closed in a timely manner in order to be paid.

Routine, proactive communication with the client and agents during the process will ensure there is no confusion on the status and completion of the loan. As your business grows and there are multiple loans underway simultaneously, you need to properly organize your routine communications program so you don't miss any client updates. Also, make sure that you are responding to any client questions or inquiries in a timely manner. Good communication goes a long way toward developing happy clients; happy clients are much more inclined to refer you.

Organizational Skills and Building a Team As You Grow

The first step in being organized is to put together a solid plan laying out the goals and metrics of your business. You don't need to necessarily reinvent the wheel, but think thoroughly where you expect your business to come from. For most of us, it will be by building relationships with real estate agents, builders, and financial planners. A great source of business is from past clients, either repeat business or referrals. Your plan should consider how you will reach and develop those relationships and how much time needs to be allocated to accomplish all of your goals.

You need to execute that plan with regard to what your referral target base might be. Allocating time for your regular activities is the next step in getting organized. Being successful as a loan officer requires that you spend time on different aspects of your business every day. This will include outreach calls, meeting with referral partners, talking with new clients, structuring deals, and responding to calls from clients or partners. With so many different activities, it's easy to get caught up with the work and not accomplish your goals of growing your business. As an example, let's say you believe that four hours a day should be allocated to business development activities. Two hours are needed to respond to calls and two hours are needed to work on loan files for new clients. Next, block out a schedule for every day and week that is consistent with your business plan. Make sure your schedule allocates the hours for each of these major activities; it is critical for your success. Planning is easy; the difficult part is following through and committing to your daily plan.

As your business grows, there will be a time where you can't keep up with both the business development activities and the work necessary to effectively handle your clients. This is a point where many loan officers get stuck. They think they have to do it all themselves and they plateau at their current level. They either slow down or avoid the prospecting activities or they cut corners and don't give appropriate attention to their clients. Either of these outcomes can harm your business, or worse, your reputation will suffer if clients' loans are not executed properly.

At the point you can't effectively manage the incoming referrals, it's time to start building a team. One with assistants and loan processors to help you execute your business plan correctly. Ideally, you will continue to spend a significant amount of your time meeting face-to-face, or otherwise, building your referral base and addressing the clients being referred to you. At the same time your team can be handling most of the processing and execution aspects of the loans. Training your team to mirror the procedures and best practices you have developed will ensure that clients are satisfied and your reputation is strengthened.

Since I started developing my team many years ago, I have several processors and assistants that help me manage my pipeline. They also organize and prioritize my daily calls and inbox. This has allowed me to originate more loans, structure my deals, and to continue to build and maintain my relationships. It also has allowed me to stay within my planned daily schedule of activities that is critical to my growth and success.

Be the Expert By Developing a Niche

By mastering the knowledge of specific products and the needs of specific types of customers, I have developed a skill set that is valuable to my customers. This helps to attract business in a particular niche. For example, the bank where I started my career in the mortgage industry was a major construction lender. I learned the construction loan products to the degree that I was confident to go out and build my builder referral base. I became the expert in that field since other loan officers weren't familiar with construction guidelines. If you can find a niche within your available product mix, you can create a referral base independent of the traditional sources.

By studying my products and the needs in the market, I've created another niche in recent years where I concentrate on investment property financing. My knowledge and training in the area of investment properties and the wide variety of investors at my company allows me to provide my customers with the right loan products to meet their investment needs. This is where I get an advantage over other loan officers in the industry.

I have some real estate companies that are among the larger Turnkey Investment property providers in a number of the metro markets around the country that consistently refer me business. These real estate companies work with investors and help them identify, acquire, and renovate the properties. Then, they either manage the properties or retain a management company for the investors. My ability to work with borrowers who want to finance up to ten properties allows me to leverage relationships that attracts multiple loans from individual borrowers.

Another aspect of becoming known as the expert in your niche is to be seen as the educator to your market. The real estate companies that I work with typically conduct seminars for investors, educating them on how to create wealth in financing single-family residential property investments. The attendees might be new investors or existing investors that want grow their real estate portfolio with additional properties. These seminars provide an overview of the opportunities in real estate investment and demonstrate how to locate, purchase, renovate, finance, and manage their properties.

Over the past year I have been invited to participate as a speaker in many of these seminars, providing my knowledge of investment property financing. This has only increased my position as the expert in the investment property financing arena. Speaking as the expert generates business opportunities with qualified investors that have financing needs.

A real key here is to find something in your product offering where you can specialize and then become an expert in serving that specific customer type. Demonstrate your expertise by speaking to the audience that you want to attract. Most of the time this is going to be on a local basis in your own market territory. Your audience could be individuals that may be interested in financing or more often the professionals that could be future referral sources. Another thing you can do to educate your audience and grow your credibility would be to create a pod-cast or a radio show that will open up the potential for listeners beyond speaking engagements.

The consistency of your marketing message is another important part of your personal branding as an expert. A presence on social media will reinforce what you are doing, so when people search online they can get a sense of your professionalism and expertise. Even when referred by a trusted advisor, many prospects will search online and look at your profile. Free social media platforms, like LinkedIn and Facebook, provide an accessible portfolio of your past work. This way, prospects looking for financing will see a number of online references backing up your reputation.

About Joe McBreen

Joe McBreen has been originating mortgages for the past fifteen years and currently ranks among the top 200 loan officers nationwide based on volume by Mortgage Executive Magazine's annual survey. He is a Vice President of Mortgage Lending for Guaranteed Rate in Chicago, Illinois. Joe typically helps first-time homebuyers, real estate investors and past clients looking to refinance.

In addition to originating mortgages for consumers in the greater Chicago area, Joe assists residential real estate investors around the United States with their rental property financing. He is also a frequent speaker at real estate investment conferences educating audiences on financing real estate investments. He is a licensed loan officer in Illinois, California, Indiana, Wisconsin, and Tennessee.

Joe was born and raised in Ireland. After graduating from college in Ireland, he moved to the United States in the mid-nineties. Joe has two daughters. They enjoy living in Chicago, close to all of the museums, parks and the accessibility to the downtown area.

For more information about Joe McBreen, visit

https://www.rate.com/joemcbreen

https://www.Facebook.com/TheMcBreenGroup

https://www.LinkedIn.com/in/JosephMcBreen

https://Twitter.com/McBreenGroup

Joe McBreen NMLS ID: 686541 CA - CA-DBO686541 - 413 0699, IL - 031.0031289 - MB.0005932, IN - 29044 - 11060, TN - 127044 - 109179, WI - 686541 - 27394BA
NMLS ID #2611 (Nationwide Mortgage Licensing System www.nmlsconsumeraccess.org) • CA - Licensed by the Department of Business Oversight, Division of Corporations under the California Residential Mortgage Lending Act Lic #4130699 • IL - Residential Mortgage Licensee - IDFPR, 122 South Michigan Avenue, Suite 1900, Chicago, Illinois, 60603, 312-793-3000, 3940 N. Ravenswood Ave., Chicago, IL 60613 #MB.0005932 • IN - Lic #11060 & #10332 • TN - Lic #109179 • WI - Lic #27394BA & 2611BR

MORTGAGE STORM

JJ Mazzo

Introduction

I got my start in the real estate industry right out of high school delivering home inspection reports to real estate offices. The real estate field seemed interesting to me to build a career in and when a mortgage company opened up in my area, I was able to get a job taking applications for a top producing refinancing call center. I started with absolutely no training or experience and I focused solely on leads that we purchased from the Internet. After several years I built up some great volume, doing between $24 million and $30 million per year, just off of leads. Unfortunately, the real estate market crashed around 2009 and there was a brutal shakeout among all of the businesses related to the real estate field. The companies that my wife and I were working for went under, and we went through some very difficult financial times.

In 2011 I was discussing the mortgage industry with one of my former mentors and he showed me how I needed to completely change how I was approaching the business. Instead of working strictly off of Internet leads and making 150 to 200 calls a day, he suggested that I should be getting out and meeting people in person. That was something that I had thought about and I wanted to do, but at that point hadn't been doing. I began to change my business model and started holding educational classes for agents, providing some value to them. I was still working with the leads to bring in income, but I was also getting out, as much as possible in my spare time to build relationships. I was probably working about 70 to 80 hours every week at that point. Around the Christmas holiday period, my father was very ill in the hospital and I was working from his room to be nearby. I turned off my leads and a magical thing happened. The phone kept ringing, but the calls were from the agent relationships I had been building. I never had to turn on the leads again. Over a fairly short time I was able to transform my business model from 100% refinancing with Internet leads to 90% purchase loans and with 100% referred business. Last year I originated $138 million in loans this way.

I've now been in the mortgage industry for nearly twenty years and am a senior loan officer and branch manager with Summit Funding in San Juan Capistrano, California. My team and I originate loans throughout the Orange County area. I'm also coaching other loan officers around the country with The CORE Training, one of the top real estate and mortgage coaching companies in the country.

Common Obstacles for Loan Officers

Compliance Requirements Have Created a Barrier to Entry

The compliance aspect of our business has quadrupled since I got into the business. Compliance relates to what people and companies in the mortgage industry can and cannot do— basically the regulatory mandates—and all of the licensing requirements. These have become much more difficult than when I was starting out. It's not just the barriers to entry, but a lot of people in our business have left the industry, because these barriers also affect the ability to stay in the business. Now, that can actually be a good thing, because if you can get in, there's less competition than there once was, and there's also more income potential than there once was.

Many Loan Officers Get Stuck Because They Are Not Leveraging With a Team

After achieving some level of success, many loan officers still try to do everything by themselves, so they're not effectively leveraging their time. Mortgage origination is a self-generation business and you can't do it all if you want to build a large volume. The more you produce, then the harder it is to maintain customer service levels. We teach in The CORE Training that you need one support staff person to assist you for every five loans you are processing per month, in addition to a loan processor. So for example, if you intend to average twenty loan originations per month, you would need four staff people assisting you plus a processor. Besides effectively servicing the clients in escrow, loan officers need to be prospecting consistently for new business. Building a team around you will help you get everything done and take you to the next levels.

Building and growing your business team requires constant tweaking and improvements as your business expands in order to maintain service levels. If you're doing a great job, it's impossible not to grow. I believe that the only way you don't grow is if you just do an average job, so you will likely see below average referrals. You need to make sure that you are wowing all of your clients. You can't please everyone all of the time, but you can sure try.

Policies regarding who pays for staff vary from company-to-company and possibly on the volume of business that loan officers deliver. Even if, as a loan officer, you're paying for staff on your own, it still makes absolute sense to have the support you need to grow. What doesn't make sense is that someone who should be making three hundred dollars per hour would be doing work that someone that makes twenty dollars per hour can do. Hire people to help you with the regular work and focus your time on the most valuable work, like prospecting for new business.

Value of Mentoring and Coaching

One of best ways to get started on your path to success as a mortgage originator is to align with a successful loan officer, one that is willing to train you and show you the path. In my first jobs assisting loan officers, I was able to work for some officers that honestly showed me the important aspects of this business and how we have to be accountable. As I got older, the business owners—the CEO's of the mortgage companies I was affiliated with—mentored me at an even higher level.

Coaching is another area where I have benefited tremendously. I received coaching through The CORE Training. They not only helped me with improving my origination business, but they also changed my life. I learned the importance of giving, the importance of saving, and the importance of sharing the path forward with others in our industry. Now I'm able to take what I have learned and share it with other loan officers who are either starting out or that want to grow their business, but just don't know how. I'm able to give them the tools to help them succeed, and I have to say that it's gratifying to me beyond words to be able to help.

Keys to Success As a Mortgage Originator

Have the Proper Mindset

Like sales people in most industries, loan officers need to have positive mindset focused on winning and a drive to work hard. People who focus on the negative and make excuses are not likely to get very far.

This can be a very financially rewarding business, but it does take a lot of hard work to succeed. When you learn new systems or strategies, or have some ideas to improve, don't procrastinate; rapid implementation is always critical for success.

184

Another important characteristic is to maintain a sense of humility. What I have found is that humility goes a long way in connecting with clients; but based on my observations, many loan officers are not humble. With humility, clients can relate to you and you appear authentic, which earns their trust and their business. Remember that this also applies to those who work for you, as they likely have a lot of contact with your clients.

Be Consistent With Prospecting and Building Relationships

Many originators spend too much key time working on the loans themselves and they're not doing enough talking with prospects and building relationships. They get stuck in the business and the loans, and that's not the highest and best use of their time. For originators to be successful and really blow up the volume, they need to be out there building relationships—making it rain. If you're relatively new, you may not have so many loans to process, so you have put enough effort into prospecting. If your volume has grown to the point where you can't handle it all without ramping down the prospecting, you need to have the staff to support the clients you have brought in.

I believe loan officers need to be consistently spending 20 to 30 hours a week prospecting and building their relationships, even if they have already built a successful business. In order to build relationships with agents and other referral sources, you need to consistently be contacting them on the phone, you need to meet them face-to-face, and you need to have meals with them. I've found a great way to build relationships is by sponsoring leveraged events, where we can see many people all at once. These events can take many different forms, such as seminars where you're educating people, happy hours, and other social events.

Even though I'm achieving a very high volume, I still don't veer from putting in the effort and doing the things that got me to where I am. I consistently do my power hours, calling as many people as I can. With the good old-fashioned phone calls, I can quickly describe my unique value proposition, hear agents' pains and show how we solve all of their needs. I consistently do my events and make sure that I connect with the agents I've been working with for a long time as well as the new agents. I stay in contact with thank you cards and small random personalized gifts just to show my appreciation.

All of this allows me to produce even more. If you're not out prospecting, just waiting for the business to come to you, it's complacency. Complacency is the death of business. If you see more people and talk to more people than everybody else, you're going to get more results than everybody else. One thing to remember is that you always have to ask for the business. You may have a fifty-fifty shot of getting the business if you ask. You have a one hundred percent chance of not getting the business if you don't ask for it.

Branding and Differentiation

In this business, there really aren't lots of differences in programs and rates from lender-to-lender. If we want to be a leader in our market we have to find a way to stand out. In my opinion, this can be done through branding and differentiation on a service model, making sure you have something that separates you from the crowded field.

We found a way to offer a level of service that solved a common problem in our local area that is unmatched by others in our market. Starting around 2012, we noticed that there were a lot of cash buyers for properties and my clients needing financing couldn't compete with the cash offers due to the traditional closing period. To solve this we came up with a quick-close process. We reverse engineered the entire loan processing and closing to be able to close within just 15 days and we can now even offer a 10-day guaranteed close. Since we were able to do it over and over again, interest really grew among agents here in

Orange County. We developed branding and advertising around the fast close guarantee. We developed unique ads and ideas to make sure that we let the agents know that's what we do and it's kind of snowballed. We are able to offer the 10-day close on about 90% of our individual loan products and 30% of our closings last year were done in fifteen days or less. Other lenders may be able to execute a fast close on an exception basis, but they generally don't like to do it and they really hope agents don't hear about it, because it takes a lot of extra staff and effort. We took a different approach, built a brand around the fast close, and market it widely.

Our creating and sponsorship of real estate related events is another part of our branding. While typically you will see mortgage companies sponsoring these events, our team itself also is a frequent sponsor, so our team is there sponsoring right alongside entire mortgage companies. Thinking big is important to me. We've gotten to the point where we even have our own large events. We have established an annual Oktoberfest for real estate agents in Orange County and a Casino Night for agents as well. The proceeds go to charity and these events draw a large crowd of agents. Most importantly, we are the face of these events and this just perpetuates our superior branding in the Orange County market.

Master the Business By Doing It

There's neither a book nor a college you can go to learn the mortgage business. This is truly a business of "hard knocks." You need to start at the bottom and work your way up. You can start as a dialer, on the phones making calls for a producing loan officer. Next, you learn how to become an application taker. The next logical step is learning how to put the loan files together. You can then advance to a junior loan officer, where you're learning to incorporate all of those skills, as well as going out and building relationships, utilizing the producing loan officer's team to get the loans processed. Ultimately, you will learn to become a loan officer yourself. The best way to learn is by doing all aspects of the business. I don't think there's a better way.

Being a loan officer is not for everyone, because there's a lot of risk involved and income is 100% commission based. Many people do fail for a variety of reasons, so some people find themselves very content in a loan officer's assistant position. I spent about the first five years of my career, in one way, shape, or form as support staff. I probably wouldn't have done it any differently, because I really learned the business this way.

Time Blocking to Make Sure You Are Getting Your Important Work Done

Unless we carefully plan how we spend our time, we won't use it well, and it will be difficult to get the important work done. I have found that time blocking is an important concept to control the time in each and every day, instead of letting something else take control of you and your time. I talked earlier about the need to focus time for prospecting and relationship building. I block this time as well as time for problem solving, power hours and coaching. All of these activities are blocked into my days first so I know I will be getting these crucial tasks completed. I have open time to meet with clients and those slots are to get filled. My marketing events and leveraged events are already booked out a whole year in advance. Each day I know exactly where I'm going and what I'm doing. Then, when it's time to leave at the end of the day, I know that I've accomplished everything that I needed to do. No matter what level you're at, you need to get a level of consistency and grab ahold of your day instead of your day grabbing ahold of you. The only way to do that is by time blocking.

Invest in Coaching

The mortgage business is not easy; it's a very high impact, high intensity business. If you like that type of thing, then this business is for you. The reason it pays well is because there are a lot of moving parts and there can be a lot of chaos that all needs to be controlled. You have to be able to keep your balance and focus on what matters. That's where I think that investing in coaching can make a big difference in speeding up your business and personal success.

There are many coaching models available and I would suggest that as you are choosing a coaching program and a coach, you find someone that will hold you accountable. If you just want some good advice, and you don't really want to be held accountable, you can just read a book, but it's not going to give you the same results. When you know what to do and you are held accountable for taking action, results and changes in you will happen.

In our coaching program we connect in a small group via videoconference every two weeks, where everyone can share what they are doing and be transparent. All participants must buy into accountability. We also see each other every six months face-to-face for four days. There is a lot of sharing of what's working and we find everyone grows through the process. The hardest part for some people is surrendering to a process. You need to be coachable and you need to implement systems and tactics quickly. You have to look at who is coaching you and if they are more successful than you are, they make more money, they're doing more loans, you need to listen to what they are saying and model what they are doing.

About JJ Mazzo

JJ Mazzo is a Scotsman's Guide and Mortgage Executive Magazine nationally ranked Top 100 producing Sr. Loan Officer with Summit Funding, Inc. He is a Producing Branch Manager for Summit Funding's branch in San Juan Capistrano, California. With his two decades of experience, he has expert knowledge in all facets of the home loan process. He and his team originate mortgages in Orange County, California.

His focus on speed, marketing and a commitment to customer satisfaction has earned him Five Star mortgage professional customer service awards for the past three years. JJ was the first in Orange County to create the ten-day escrow close guarantee. This allows borrowers to have the same advantage as cash buyers when competing for an accepted offer on a home purchase.

His leadership, as a branch manager with streamlined processes and experienced staff, allows him to offer a per diem guarantee should him not close a loan on time. Additionally, he is a business coach and is personally coached as a top member of The CORE Training, one of the country's top mortgage and real estate coaching firms. His obligation to share with others for success separates him from the rest.

JJ resides in San Juan Capistrano with his wife and two beautiful daughters and is a member of the Orange County Association of Realtors®. He is a committed sponsor of CHOC Children's Hospital of Orange County, Orange County Rescue Mission, and a member of Giveback Homes.

For more information on JJ Mazzo, visit

www.TheMazzoGroup.com

MORTGAGE STORM

Manuel Corral

....

Introduction

When I was eighteen years old I was working in a warehouse and was taking college courses at night. I knew that I wanted to do something where I could make some good money and I thought college was going to take too long. I decided to try real estate and I got my real estate license and started working in the field as an agent at only nineteen years of age. Back when I started, banks were the primary place to get a mortgage, so I picked up a lot of mortgage applications from the banks to help my clients that were going to need financing.

Back then, as real estate agents, we would help the clients fill out the loan applications and then turn them into the bank representatives assigned for our area. Within a few short years I was selling a lot of houses and in one year I turned in 32 applications to one of the banks. A loan officer recognized that I was bringing in lots of loans into the bank and she indicated that I would make a good loan officer. She said that in two years at the bank I would have the equivalent of a four-year college degree. I interviewed with the bank and four months later accepted a position as a loan officer. I quickly found out what hard work was. In the first month I wrote forty-three loan applications.

I've now been in the mortgage industry for thirty-one years and I am the production manager for Golden Empire Mortgage's Pomona, California office. My team and I originate mortgages in the East San Gabriel Valley and the Inland Empire, just east of Los Angeles and in other areas of Southern California.

Common Obstacles for Loan Officers

You Have to Go Out and Generate Your Own Business

We're all in the business of acquiring customers. When you're in the mortgage business and working as a loan officer you have to go out and get your own business. Now if you are working for a conventional bank branch, there is some walk-in business, but even there you have to go out and develop most of your own business. This can be a challenge when you are just starting and don't have an established book of business. One also has to quickly develop the knowledge and confidence to be able to convey to real estate agents you have the ability to handle their client's loans. Agents need to be convinced that the loans will be properly executed and closed on time or they risk not getting paid.

Without Detailed Knowledge of the Guidelines, You Won't Be Much Use to Customers

The mortgage business is different than most in many ways. In other industries sales people don't always have to be an expert in their products. Loan officers not only have to do the selling, but they also have to know the systems for processing the loans. Qualification standards, guidelines, and loan processing are not topics you will be able to learn in school first, so it's pretty much on-the-job learning. It's critical to learn this aspect before you start trying to bring in customers. If you can't properly qualify and process their loans you can do your customers a disservice by not being able to provide proper advice.

Value of Coaches and Training

I did very well in the business and made a lot of money in my twenties. I wasn't very wise with my money and ended up losing most of everything in my thirties. In my mid-thirties, I decided that I was going to make a comeback and really focus on building a good business. I decided to invest in myself, so I hired the Duncan Group to coach me. To this day, I am still very involved in coaching. I'm currently in an Elite Mastermind Group of twenty-four loan officers from around the country and we meet periodically, strategizing on developing best practices and systems for maximizing our businesses. I really bought into learning and implementing the best systems for my business.

One needs to become a lifelong learner in this business and with all of the resources that are out there today you can do that without having to spend a lot of money. Something I learned along the way is that you not only need to work in your business, you also need to work on your business, making it better each year. You have to dedicate yourself to study this business if you want to become a master in it. Whether it be setting up new systems, figuring out better ways to market or thinking through how to get more referral partners, you have to be improving everything you do and honing your skills every year if you want to keep advancing and growing.

One way to do this is to attend industry seminars and workshops, not one time, but every year. There are some well-known national events and you can get the opportunity to meet the top mortgage producers and coaches at these events. Believe me, when you hang out with the top producers, you learn a lot and more success generally comes with hanging out with people better than you are. I don't just go to these events on my own, I also take my key team members with me, so I'm not only investing in myself, but my teammates as well. I want them to hear the people that are coaching me and to listen to how they speak, so that we can all understand the methods and be able to speak the same business language that I speak.

I was fortunate to be able to spend some time on site visits with some of the top producing loan officers across the country. It wasn't cheap, as I had to pay to spend a day with them on top of the airfare, but it was worth every penny. I was able to tour their offices, review their business plans and see how they ran their operations. With this knowledge, I started to paint a picture of what I wanted to do in my career and business.

Investing in yourself is key. When I went to my first event, I barely had enough money in my pocket to even attend. Things are different today and I am spending about $40,000 a year on coaching for my team and me.

Keys to Success As a Mortgage Originator

Have a Positive Mindset

First of all, we need to have to have a positive mindset, a positive attitude. One needs to stay on point and not waste time every single day. I think that for me, part of my success has been because I'm extremely competitive, I'm extremely driven, and I'm extremely focused. For me, the proper mindset is the first key.

Get a Mentor

People that are new in this business likely don't have much direction. It is recommended to initially work under someone who has already achieved success building the business as a loan officer. If you can find the right mentor to work under you will learn how to do this business and you can model what your mentor is doing. I would recommend working with a top producing loan officer as part of a team and you will be able to learn many aspects of the business from how to quality a client, to the best ways to develop a referral source base, and how to provide clients with a valuable service. It's important to work with someone who is doing a considerable volume of loans on a regular basis, say at least fifteen per month, so you can be exposed to a large number of situations in as fast a time as possible. Within a year or two you will likely be able to learn enough to go out on your own. Looking back over my career, one of the things that specifically catapulted me was that I surrounded myself with a lot of people that took an interest in my career and actually guided me through the process.

Master Your Lending Guidelines to Become an Expert

When I started in the business, most of the mortgages in California were done by a number of large Savings and Loan Banks. I went to work for the largest one and it was known for having the best training program in the industry. They would send us to a boot camp for about two weeks and we would learn about their products and role-play for selling their programs. There is not much internal training like this available today, so on-the-job training is going to be the key. You cannot be an effective loan officer today unless you have mastered the guidelines. Start with the most common programs, which are the conventional FHA and VA loans, depending on your marketplace. If you're not well versed on these, you're going to be exposed in this business.

As a lender, you have to position yourself to be the expert. You have to be able to speak intelligently to real estate agents and borrowers about the guidelines. Agents are primarily looking to work with people that have the correct answers. It's that simple and straightforward. If you're going to sit down with a client and advise them, you better know what you're talking about. Too many lenders waste the time of their clients or referring agents because they really don't know how to properly advise or qualify a client.

I use my knowledge and experience to make the loan process a value-added service for my clients. It's really more than just filling out a form and processing the loan. I want to coach my customers and be able to send them out with a game plan to work with their real estate agent who is now going to execute the transaction. Being able to properly educate clients is critical. You have to learn how to properly present payment options and solutions to buyers, to help them make the best decisions for their families.

I have a six-step process to make sure clients get the right loan for their individual situation. When a client wants to apply for a loan, I'll either have a phone call or an in person meeting to make sure I understand their needs and goals. First, I'm going to get a good picture of the income. Next I'm going to analyze the credit based on credit score, obligations, and ability to pay. Third, I want to understand how much money has been set aside for a down payment and funds to close. Next I want to understand the client's payment goals. Fifth, I also try to understand the client's core values and long-term goals. The sixth step is to make sure there is clarity on the client's expectations. Finally, when I have all of this information and have provided a professional consultation, I think I can meet or exceed my clients' needs. That's how I've built my business, every single time, with every single client.

Build Up a Base of Referral Partners

For most of us we need to build up a network of referral partners to send us leads. Real estate agents are one of the most important typical sources, but others could include CPAs, financial advisors, and insurance agents. Since I started out in real estate as an agent, I have an affinity with other agents, so I have pretty much focused on them. It takes time and it doesn't happen overnight. Very few people can come out of the blocks fresh in the industry and bring in twenty or thirty loans a month. It doesn't happen that way. You have to build a reputation and you have to build your business, one referral source and one client at a time.

Acquiring real estate agents as partners is not an easy thing to do. If you want to acquire agents, you have to go where the agents are hanging out. You have to go to the agent seminars, the local real estate board's meetings, and maybe the open houses to introduce yourself. Open houses might be the only opportunity to meet them one-on-one. Once you get an opportunity from a new source, you have to score a touchdown; you can't fumble the ball on the way to the goal line. This is where knowing the guidelines and the loan programs is crucial.

When I first meet with a real estate agent, I want to do what's called a high trust interview. I want to meet the agent one-on-one. Getting the initial meeting is the hardest part, but there's a tactic that I use that works well for me. I'm really looking for weaknesses and gaps in the agent's business. I then analyze those gaps and provide the agent with solutions on how to close the gaps in their business. If I can provide some valuable advice, now I've become a solution provider. I use this to gain their respect and to acquire their business. We need to remember that we're in a job of getting the agents paid and our number one goal is to deliver a happy client. A happy client is going to give them referrals. It's going to be a reflection on me, so I have to make sure I do good work.

Develop a Niche or Specialty and Master It

For a loan officer starting out I would recommend to create a niche or specialty focus and to master the skills necessary to become an expert in the focus area. An example of a specialty could be first-time homebuyers. Another focus could be the Fannie Mae and Freddie Mac conventional loan products. These conventional loans are very formulistic and you can fine tune your skills and master the guidelines fairly quickly. Once you've mastered a specialty, you can go out and target referral partners and prospects that match your focus expertise and need to be served. At the same time master your presentation skills, not just for the agent interviews, but also for when you are in the office presenting to clients.

Keep in Contact With Past Clients as They Will Need Another Loan at Some Point and They Can Refer Others

I see a lot of originators that don't keep in contact with their clients. Your client is someone that you have already done business with, and if you have a good business model, providing good service, your clients should already know, like, and trust you. Why not stay positioned in their mind by keeping in contact? At some point they will need another loan, rates will be lower so they could benefit from a refinance, and they will know people buying a house that need a loan. We put all of our customers into a database and we are contacting them at least once a month with some kind of touch. We use emails, newsletters and provide information on the market. By doing this we are "top of mind" when they need another loan or one of their friends or relatives is shopping for a house.

Build A Team to Leverage Your Total Volume

One sticking point for experienced originators is that they achieve a good level of success but they hit a barrier because they don't have time to grow any further. What I observe is that they will be working sixty or seventy or more hours a week but they are stuck at the same level. They are in a state of chaos and getting pulled on every few minutes by someone. At this point, the best advice is to start developing a team to help you, even if you have to personally pay your team. Most people are cautious when adding staff due to the inherent risks involved, but it is amazing the power of leverage when you strategically start to build a team.

A number of years ago, I was quite successful, but just couldn't expand my volume for three years in a row, despite working very hard. I decided to begin to add staff and hired an assistant and a marketing person. The following year I doubled my business, even though I was laid up after an auto accident and had to miss three months of work. It shows the power of leveraging through a team. An assistant can elevate your performance to a completely new level if you hire the right person. John Maxwell, one of my favorite authors, said, "If you have Mount Everest dreams, you need a Mount Everest team."

Develop an Impeccable Reputation

You have to build your reputation and honor your word, one transaction at a time. You can't hide from phone calls. When they make a mistake, too many lenders don't return the client's or agent's calls. You cannot hide from the phone call; you have to run to the call. The other thing is you have to deliver on your promises. You only have one chance to impress. When you get that opportunity, you have to make sure that you going to score points.

About Manuel Corral

Manuel Corral is a thirty-one year veteran of the mortgage industry and the leader of the Golden Empire Mortgage branch in Pomona, California. He and his team originate mortgages in the in the East San Gabriel Valley and the Inland Empire, just east of Los Angeles and other areas of Southern California. Manuel is a perennial member of Golden Empire's Chairman's Circle and an eight-time winner of the company's top producing loan officer award. He has been nationally recognized as a top performer by several mortgage publications such as The Scotsman's Guide, Mortgage Executive Magazine, and Mortgage Originator Magazine and was awarded NAHREP's top Latino Originator Award for 2014 and was No. 2 in 2015. Manual has closed over 3500 loans totaling over $900,000,000 in the past 15 years.

Manuel believes strongly in having a personal coach, a business coach, and strong mentors. He credits his success to his belief in God, his family, and his many mentors and business associates. He believes in people before profits and reputation before revenue. He is a frequent speaker and has spoken at the Real Estate and Mortgage Mastermind Summit over many years as well at Duncan Group's Sales Mastery Events.

For more information about Manuel Corral, visit

http://www.ManuelCorral.com

https://www.facebook.com/GoldenEmpireMortgage

https://www.linkedin.com/in/manuelcorral

http://www.zillow.com/profile/Manuel-Corral

http://www.yelp.com/biz/Golden-Empire-Mortgage-Pomona-2

CPSIA information can be obtained
at www.ICGtesting.com
Printed in the USA
LVHW081111060222
710393LV00020B/431